D1631176

Gig

Gig

The Life and Times of a Rock-star Fantasist

SIMON ARMITAGE

VIKING
an imprint of
PENGUIN BOOKS

821.914
ARM

VIKING

Published by the Penguin Group

Penguin Books Ltd, 80 Strand, London WC2R 0RL, England
Penguin Group (USA) Inc., 375 Hudson Street, New York, New York 10014, USA
Penguin Group (Canada), 90 Eglinton Avenue East, Suite 700, Toronto, Ontario, Canada M4P 2Y3
(a division of Pearson Penguin Canada Inc.)
Penguin Ireland, 25 St Stephen's Green, Dublin 2, Ireland (a division of Penguin Books Ltd)
Penguin Group (Australia), 250 Camberwell Road, Camberwell, Victoria 3124, Australia
(a division of Pearson Australia Group Pty Ltd)
Penguin Books India Pvt Ltd, 11 Community Centre, Panchsheel Park, New Delhi – 110 017, India
Penguin Group (NZ), 67 Apollo Drive, Rosedale, North Shore 0632, New Zealand
(a division of Pearson New Zealand Ltd)
Penguin Books (South Africa) (Pty) Ltd, 24 Sturdee Avenue, Rosebank, Johannesburg 2196, South Africa

Penguin Books Ltd, Registered Offices: 80 Strand, London WC2R 0RL, England

www.penguin.com

First published 2008
1

Copyright © Simon Armitage, 2008

The moral right of the author has been asserted

All photographs appear courtesy of Simon Armitage, except the two 'Surtsey' photos © Tim Dee;
'Simon and Craig in Studio' © Duncan McKenzie, and 'A Reading in Yorkshire' © Jonty Wilde.

All rights reserved
Without limiting the rights under copyright
reserved above, no part of this publication may be
reproduced, stored in or introduced into a retrieval system,
or transmitted, in any form or by any means (electronic, mechanical,
photocopying, recording or otherwise), without the prior
written permission of both the copyright owner and
the above publisher of this book

Set in 14.25/16.75pt Monotype Dante
Typeset by Rowland Phototypesetting Ltd, Bury St Edmunds, Suffolk
Printed in Great Britain by Clays Ltd, St Ives plc

A CIP catalogue record for this book is available from the British Library

ISBN: 978–0–670–91580–4

www.greenpenguin.co.uk

Penguin Books is committed to a sustainable future
for our business, our readers and our planet.
The book in your hands is made from paper
certified by the Forest Stewardship Council.

for Speedy Sue (of Sue and the Speedy Bears fame)

gig *n. & v. colloq:* **1** a musical performance; **2** an engagement for an entertainer; **3** a job of work.

Contents

Contents

Acknowledgements

A version of 'Rock of Ages' first appeared in *'Do You, Mr Jones?' Bob Dylan with the Poets and Professors*, edited by Neil Corcoran (Chatto & Windus, 2002). A version of 'On the Road 1' first appeared in *Mortification: Writers' Stories of their Public Shame*, edited by Robin Robertson (Fourth Estate, 2004). Acknowledgements are also due to the magazines and newspapers in which extracts from various pieces first appeared.

Gig

I've only been involved with books and writing for the second half of my life, but music has been around from day one. Growing up in the Armitage family there was barely a minute's silence. Mum continued to play the piano even after someone had lifted the lid and vomited into it during a birthday party, and on Friday nights I witnessed a peculiar transformation in my dad as he glued mutton chop facial hair to the side of his face and went off to sing in a hotel in Ashton-under-Lyne with his barber's shop group the Victorians. They wore extravagant waistcoats made from a furry patterned fabric reminiscent of the heavy flock wallpaper once favoured by Indian restaurants and the function rooms of working men's clubs. The waistcoats were a plum and burgundy colour, but they also owned several other sets in equally lavish colours which served as away kits when the first choice bibs were at the dry-cleaner's. The Victorians rehearsed in our house every Sunday morning, a handful of them making the china in the sideboard chatter and ring with their close harmonies. Upstairs in bed I'd watch the light fitting tremble, and feel the bedsprings buzz with the deep vibration of some hunting medley or heartfelt serenade.

My own musical career began at age eight in a junior school concert. One case of mumps and one case of truancy on the day of the performance resulted in my hasty promotion from the wooden blocks to the triangle, then from the triangle to the drum. Which shouldn't have been a big deal, except that the piece to be performed was 'The Little Drummer Boy'. So instead of goofing around at the back with the other numpties and non-musicians I was suddenly thrust into the spotlight as the sweet-smiling hero of the song's title. Things began well enough, but I lost the rhythm in the second verse, when instead of concentrating I began looking for the approving faces of my parents in the audience. Before I had a chance to recover, the drum was commandeered by the commandeering Mrs Bond, who set about trying to restore the beat. She of all people should have known better than to give me the instrument in the first place. She was a friend of the family, and the family had set a poor precedent in the percussion department. My great-grandfather played the big bass drum in the village band. The job required a man with a strong back, which he had, but he was not particularly tall. One year, bringing up the rear of the procession during the annual parade, and unable to see over the top of his instrument, as the rest of the band forked right towards the river Jack Armitage marched onwards up Peel Street, hammering out his rhythm until it was the only sound bouncing back and forth between the shop windows and the dark, high walls of the Mechanics' Institute. Musically speaking, I probably have more in common with Jack than with any other of my relatives, alive or dead.

I was head boy in the village choir for a few years, playing three-card brag and scabby queen behind the choir stalls while our weird vicar, Father James, prostrated himself in front of the altar and offered his body to God. When my voice broke I was sent for piano lessons with the patient and house-proud Mrs Mickelthwaite. In response to me turning up on her doorstep straight from football practice with bloody knees and muddy boots, she would carefully line her hallway and living room with newspapers or magazines, and would even lay a centrefold page of the *Huddersfield Examiner* across the piano stool. After half an hour of clunky, sweaty piano playing, I'd walk home with columns of local news imprinted on the back of my bare thighs. I haven't sung much in my adult life, one exception being my rendition of Lou Reed's 'Perfect Day', broadcast on BBC Radio 3 and recorded at a lonely farmhouse in Iceland, accompanied by the poet Glyn Maxwell playing the piano on which the Icelandic national anthem was composed. It seemed to make sense at the time.

Apart for my cousin's Supertramp albums and the tinnitus of daytime Radio 1, music was a kind of background drone for a few years, until I tuned in to the *John Peel Show*. Almost immediately I became a punk. Not a proper fuck-off punk with a cockatoo hairdo and DESTROY tattooed across his forehead, but a Marsden punk in replica oxblood Docs, his sister's baggy jumper and a pair of tartan kecks left over from an Operatic Society performance of *Brigadoon*. I once went a step further, constructing a pair of bondage trousers using the straps from an old tent, though running for the bus through the streets of a northern mill village in such constrictive legwear had little to recommend it.

Undeterred, I told everyone I'd been to see the Sex Pistols playing their last ever UK gig at Ivanhoe's Nightclub in Huddersfield. I hadn't. I was too scared. We were all too scared. In fact if everyone in Huddersfield claiming to have been at that legendary gig had actually been there, the venue would have exceeded its capacity by some twenty thousand.

The punk phase didn't last long but I was obviously still under the influence on my eighteenth birthday. I don't suppose it was too unusual for young men who were coming of age in the early eighties to have the signs and symbols of their current obsession emblazoned in coloured icing sugar on top of a big cake. A football badge, perhaps, or maybe something in the shape of a McLaren F1. But did anyone else out there have, as a cake decoration, a perfect facsimile of the cenotaph-style cover of the Siouxsie and the Banshees album *Join Hands*, with its four monochrome soldiers, its carved lettering and its commemorative poppy motif? To her credit, Mum embraced the whole concept (i.e. gave me enough rope) and put the cake on prominent display on the kitchen table with the actual album propped up behind. She completed the configuration with a bunch of red roses which looked like they'd been borrowed from a war memorial or stolen from a grave. My father's response is not recorded in my memory, or has been unconsciously deleted. At the party aunts, uncles and friends of the family filed mournfully past the cake in silence, paying their respects.

After punk I was a mod. A Marsden mod. There were three of us. We went down to the Army and Navy Stores and got kitted out with fishtail parkas. My mate's sister ironed a bullseye target on the back of his. I hand-stitched a fox-tail on to the bottom of mine but tucked it inside the lining before I got home every night. On bank holidays we stood outside Marsden fire station on the A62 giving the thumbs-up to the convoys of scooters en route to Blackpool on the west coast or returning from Bridlington to the east. The buffed chrome of the Vespas and Lambrettas dazzled in the sun. The hundreds of wing mirrors glittered and winked. From inside their piss-pot helmets and behind their shades, the chapters of white-socked soul boys shouted unanswerable terms of abuse, stuck up two gloved fingers at us and disappeared over the hill.

Offended but not defeated, I turned to New Romanticism. As my NUS card from 1982 will testify, I wore a silk scarf and dinner jacket combination and grew a Phil Oakey-style half-fringe which hung like a vulture's wing over one eye. In the photograph, I'm attempting to stare moodily and reflectively through that curtain of hair towards some transitory moment of beautiful sadness beyond the vision of less sensitive mortals – not easy in the photo-booth in Woolies – and despite the defacing effect of a staple, a Theatre of Hate button-badge is still visible on my left lapel. Later that year, I ordered a pair of pointy suede boots from my mum's catalogue. When they arrived, my dad ripped open the box, thinking it was his new spade head. Mum, bless her, averted a major altercation by pretending she'd ordered them for her friend's daughter. I had to hide them in a bush down the road, leave the house each evening in a pair of Dunlop Green Flash and change my footwear beneath the shadowy leaves of a rhododendron bush before getting the train to Manchester or Leeds and leaving muddy footprints on the dance floors of some of the North's best nightclubs. My enthusiasm for synthesizer music and billowing pattern-print blouses was tolerated by my father because he knew it would be short-lived. After all, I was still playing sport for the village; a New Romantic wouldn't last long among the jockstraps and Brut of the football changing rooms or on the cricket field at the edge of the moor, amidst the sheep droppings and hailstones. I was still drinking at Pule Side Working Men's Club; a Russian hussar's jacket and a pair of riding britches weren't going to cut much ice in there.

I formed several bands with my mates, most of which never played a note. I've always carried a special memory of one of those bands, a thrash-punk outfit called Tess and the d'Urbs, whipping up a mini-riot in the sixth form common room at the end of term. But a photograph of that 'gig' came to light recently, and as well as being disturbed to see how much lipstick and eyeliner I was wearing, I noted with some disappointment that our guitars were made out of cardboard. I've also mouthed off many times about a band I once played in called the Fabrics, with Terry Towelling on drums, Poly Ester doing backing vocals, Ray On playing bass and me – singer-songwriter Bri Nylon – howling into the microphone and strangling a Fender Strat. But there was no such band. I made the whole thing up.

In fact my wife has more claim to rock-and-roll credibility than I have, with a business card to prove it. During her years at Leicester University she fronted a folk-rock outfit which went under the rather fantastic name of Sue and the Speedy Bears. The bear in question is pictured on the aforementioned card in what appears to me to be a mind-altered state, strumming a guitar and wearing a pair of shades. When the band were interviewed by Radio Leicestershire, her parents drove up from London so they could park inside the country boundary and listen to the broadcast. Sometimes, when we want a good laugh, she pulls out the *Speedy Sue Song Book* (i.e. a jotter full of handwritten lyrics) or even puts on a C45 Speedy Sue

SPEEDY BEARS

Holbrook Road
South Knighton
Leicester

demo tape. But although it's hilarious, it's more than I've got to show. Because for all the musical posturing and attitude of my early life, my entire back catalogue amounts to precisely nothing.

When I was nineteen I had my ear pierced. I was away at college at the time, and at the end of term I made the journey home by bus, the train being too expensive. To combat the travel sickness caused by seven hours on a National Express coach I dropped a couple of Sea-Legs tablets and washed them down with a can of Guinness before boarding, then spent most of the journey in a semi-comatose state, gawping out of the window, counting lamp posts. I was still only partly conscious when Huddersfield bus station slewed into view. My parents were waiting in one of the bays. Mum spotted the earring and ushered me into the car to avoid a confrontation, or at least to delay it, because short of wearing a balaclava for the whole summer, the silver ring inserted through my left ear lobe was going to become visible at some point. In fact Dad had also clocked it, but had made an instant decision to plot his revenge rather than fly off the handle. A couple of days later when I walked into the club I was met with wolf whistles, limp-wristed hand gestures and a beery chorus of 'All the Nice Boys Love a Sailor'. Dad just shrugged his shoulders and raised his drink to his mouth, as if suggesting the local tribe's reaction to my act of self-mutilation was entirely spontaneous and beyond his control. But through the optical distortion of his pint glass, his smile was magnified. I also suspected him of priming my grandmother's response to the earring: 'You look like a pirate,' she said about a week later, over Sunday dinner. It was intended as a double insult. Not only had I crossed the north–south divide to continue my education in a Hampshire naval city, but I had also crossed over to the darker side of seamanship. When me and Dad finally got around to having something like an adult conversation about the earring, it concluded with him raising his arms to the heavens and exclaiming, 'OK, but what does it mean?' He was probably thinking that the men of the Armitage family had lived for hundreds of years, surviving many wars and protecting their precious blood through conflict and battle, only for the last male in the line to voluntarily breach his own flesh for the sake of ornamentation.

I didn't know what the earring meant. At some level I thought it might make me an angry young man. But a guy I really admired at the time had, according to rumours, pierced both of his nipples and also his foreskin and, when feeling particularly assertive, wore a chain connecting all three points of anchorage. By comparison he was very angry indeed. Furious, in fact. Also, my piercing had taken place in a comfy chair in the back of a jeweller's shop, with antiseptic and a box of tissues to hand, whereas really cool people did it themselves. Like most things in the eighties, this usually took place in a call box at the end of the road. The trick was to clamp the ear lobe between two cubes of ice (from the refrigeration unit in the phone box, obviously), then push a safety pin through the skin, then wear the safety pin. Since the advent of the mobile phone and the demise of the public payphone, I've often wondered where the youth of today go to puncture their skin, apply their tattoos and lose their virginity.

But a couple of years later I had worse news for my father. Much more serious; not a fad this time. It was the confession that all red-blooded fathers dread as they sense the words forming on the lips of their sons. My Adam's apple bobbed in my throat. There was no easy way of saying it. I swallowed, stared at a point on the floor somewhere between his feet and muttered, 'Dad, I think I'm a poet.' He returned to the cricket section of the

Yorkshire Post to privately calculate the effect on the family and consider his response. Perhaps he wasn't worried because he saw it as a bit of a hollow threat. After all, at that stage I had nothing to support my statement other than a few scribblings in a Silvine notebook bought from the post office, and certainly nothing published. That didn't happen until 13 August 1987. At least that's the date on the cheque sent to me from the magazine *Other Poetry*, based in Leicester. It's for the princely sum of £2.00, and

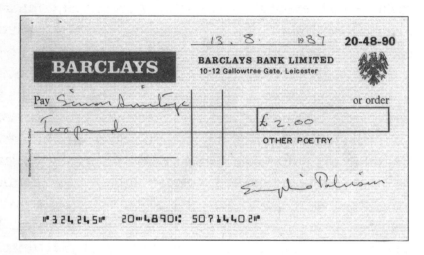

I never cashed it. For me, having work accepted by that small and now defunct publication meant everything, and nothing else has ever been quite as exciting or satisfying as appearing in print that very first time. I think it's because going from zero to something represents an increase of infinite proportions.

And yet music has been just as important to me as literature. I may own more poems than I do songs, but the songs have given me at least as much pleasure, if not more. Latterly, I've spent time in the music business: I've written libretti and I've interviewed pop stars; I've written songs for rock bands and rap lyrics for murderers; I've reviewed albums and presented programmes about popular music; I've even received an Ivor Novello Award, pushing past Bono, a pretty homunculus who turned out to be Kylie, and the lost and bewildered Brian Wilson in the glittery ballroom of the Grosvenor House Hotel to collect the gong. But the time has come to face up to a reality which eventually dawns on a great many music lovers at a certain time of life, namely that I am a failed rock star. Furthermore, it has recently occurred to me that only through the process of failing to become a rock star have I become a writer. A very particular kind of writer, that is: a poet. I don't record singles and albums; I write poems and I write books. And I don't do concerts, smashing my guitar into a hundred reverberating pieces before swallow-diving over the footlights to be caught and carried in the upraised arms of devoted fans. I give readings. I travel to venues and I write out a set list. I take a drink in the green room and wait in the wings. Occasionally I'm introduced by a chairperson or organizer, but not always. I walk on stage, sometimes towards a microphone and sometimes even into the glow of a spotlight. Then I open my mouth and do my stuff. Readings can be touching and poignant, or they can be pointless and humiliating. A single human voice speaking a considered thought can feel like the high point of human achievement, or it can feel like an object lesson in embarrassment. But whatever the poetry reading is or isn't, it's the closest I'm ever going to get to standing in front of an audience with a band behind me and a guitar in my hands. And I suspect that promoters of literary events also nurse a secret desire to be organizing Glastonbury rather than the Ledbury Poetry Festival, or chopping out cocaine on a mirror rather than filling a Tupperware bowl with Mini Cheddars, or introducing David Bowie at Wembley Arena rather than Simon Armitage in Marsden church hall. Because invariably – and often without any hint of irony to act as a necessary counterbalance – they refer to the contemporary poetry reading as a 'gig'.

Oasis
McAlpine Stadium Huddersfield
25 July 1995

Cancelled.

Review of Huddersfield Contemporary Music
Festival, *New York Times*, 2002

'This is not the most God-forsaken, grim or desolate city
in Britain, but it gives the main contenders a run for their
money.'

Paul McCartney
Hallam FM Arena Sheffield
6 April 2003

The *Independent on Sunday* want to know if I can re-pen the lyrics to 'When I'm Sixty-Four', given that McCartney's eponymous birthday is fast approaching. They'd like the new lyrics to fit the old tune, so that readers would be able to sing along should they feel inclined. They can offer a fee of 500 quid; considering the original song contains fewer than 200 words, many of them repeated, they point out that the rate they offer is about ten times as much as they pay their foreign correspondents: 'And you wouldn't even have to dodge any bullets!'

I don't know what to think about the Beatles. They're monumental and amazing, of course, but I hardly ever listen to them. It's an age thing, probably. You probably had to *be* there. At the time when I started listening to popular music and the angle from which I approached it, they were the enemy, clogging up the charts and record shops long after they'd disbanded. In their dafter moments, they were only marginally less irritating than the Smurfs or the Banana Splits. They were the group who called the mums and dads on to the dance floor to jive and spin, while we flounced back to our ashtrays and alcoves in a post-punk huff. Like vegetarians who eat tuna fish, people who don't like pop music like the Beatles. In the houses of your elders and betters, you can often find a copy of *Sgt. Pepper's* or *The Blue Album* tucked between Bach and Beethoven. Tell people you can take or leave them and you get a funny look. And I've always said that I wouldn't be seen dead at a McCartney concert, but with reviews come free tickets, and where free tickets are concerned, emphatic statements about one's own mortality are recontextualized.

It's the first night of Paul's Back in the World Tour. The programme doesn't say which planet he's returned from. The Hallam FM Arena is full, although the people at the back seem so far away from the stage that their actual attendance at the concert must be called into question. Somewhat sheepishly, we're at the front. The show opens with the emergence from all parts of the hall of jobbing circus performers, last seen at the opening ceremony of the 2002 World Cup and now with time on their hands until the first day of next year's Olympic Games. Once the smoke has cleared and the stilt walkers have been helped down from their stilts, Sir Paul appears, Bruce Forsyth-style, at the back of the stage, first as a shadow, then as the man himself. Well over two hours of music follow, and there are definite highlights, including a heartfelt 'Eleanor Rigby' and a Ramones-style 'Back in the USSR' – surely one of the earliest punk songs ever recorded. The Wings stuff also sounds peculiarly modern and particularly effective. The low moments are the songs from the new album; for about quarter of an hour it feels like the plane has lost altitude and we're all waiting for our ears to pop, which they do, eventually, with 'Blackbird' and 'We Can Work It Out'.

But it's the weird and wonky moments I'm really interested in, and by my calculation there are three. The first is 'Something', played on a ukulele. Harrison was a George Formby fan apparently – aren't we all? – but it makes for a bizarre elegy. The second is Macca's attempt at an anecdote, an unrewarding story involving a massage session with an old crone in a hotel in the Far East, including mock-Japanese syllables and dodgy facial expressions. The tale gropes towards a blurred punch-line somewhere on the distant horizon that refuses to materialize. Am I allowed to say that for a cocky Scouser, McCartney does a poor line in humour, and at his corniest moments he's only one cheese football short of being Sir Cliff Richard? But the third incident of special anthropological interest is the best: Heather Mills in the orchestra pit, singing along and waving her arms like a fan. She disappears during a song dedicated to Linda; for one heart-stopping moment I wonder if she's actually making her way towards the stage, heading for the tambourine. I think I want this to happen. But three or four minutes later she's back where she was, swaying and clapping along to 'Hey Jude', the biggest song of the night by far.

'Come on, get in the mood,' shouts Speedy Sue (of Sue and the Speedy Bears fame).

'It's mum-and-dad music,' I shout back.

She shouts, 'We *are* a mum and dad.'

I raise my arms above my head and fall in line with the beat, but my heart's not in it. I'm a grumbling Bagheera in the middle of 10,000 jiving and jitterbugging Baloos. However, it's not just because I'm an awkward bastard who'd rather be listening to a bunch of nobodies going nowhere than witnessing a piece of rock and roll history. It's this song: it makes me nervous. At Colne Valley High School, to be caught doing any work, even in the sixth form common room, was seen by other pupils as a sell-out – a betrayal of religious proportions. Anyone so much as reading a book, let alone actually putting pen to paper, could expect to hear in the background a rising, bawling chorus of fellow students singing 'Hey Jude' at the top of their voices, where the Jude of the song stood for Judas, and the Judas they were singing about was you.

*

I've been back to my old school on five or six occasions, usually to read poems and talk about poetry, once to hand out prizes and certificates at the end of the year, and once to talk about *how to make something of your life*. I've also been to the school theatre a couple of times to watch the Tudge in one her dancing class concerts, pirouetting and clap-lunging on the same stage where I once played a rather rubbishy Toad in the fourth-year production of *Toad of Toad Hall*. As well as the academic subjects I chose to study at O level, I also studied drama, though the school weren't very happy about it. It was never admitted, but at that time, drama wasn't really deemed suitable for students who could read and write, and the twice-weekly classes were thought of more as cooling-off periods for troublemakers and underachievers who might otherwise be smoking on the tennis courts or lighting fires in the cloakrooms. It wasn't even a proper O level but 16 Plus, which sounded less like a qualification and more like the certification for a film containing scenes of occasional violence and moderate peril. I have my father to thank for being allowed to study drama; being a born actor and a prominent local thespian, he could see the value in such a course, even if my head of year couldn't. On the other hand, I was less grateful for another of my father's interventions. Towards the end of my 'choices' interview, with English language, English literature, maths, geography, physics, chemistry and drama already secured, I still had one selection to make. My dad said, 'Give him woodwork. If he's doing all this clever stuff, you might as well let him bash a bit of two-by-four around for a couple of hours, work off some of his frustrations.' Unfortunately for me, the teacher on the other side of the desk just happened to be the woodwork teacher, who saw himself as a quality carpenter and who did not share my father's view of woodwork as the opportunity to pulverize an innocent length of raw timber with a hammer for purely therapeutic reasons. He ticked a box and the interview was concluded. It was only when I went back to school after the summer holidays that I discovered I would not be taking woodwork classes after all, but home economics.

'I've got cooking,' I moaned to my parents.

Mum managed a partly sympathetic smile and Dad laughed.

Only two boys in the entire year took cooking, me and a lad called Mick, whose father presumably had also insulted the noble art of joinery. Upon seeing each other queuing up for that first lesson, and recognizing ourselves as males of the species, we wiped the tears from our eyes and formed a sort of unspoken resistance movement against the forces of domesticity. The main mission was to make it through two years without any other boy in the school getting wind of the fact that while they were fashioning bookshelves and designing go-carts we would be kneading dough and decorating cakes. Every Tuesday, as secretly as possible, we'd sidle along to one of the domestic science rooms (like science labs but with gas hobs instead of Bunsen burners), and later in the day we'd slink away, via the washrooms, making sure every last grain of flour was dusted from our hands and that not one telltale molecule of pastry remained beneath our fingernails. Taking pies and buns home on the school bus required an even higher level of subterfuge. One particularly nasty character from up the road once tapped the top of my biscuit tin with his penknife and said, 'So what have you got in there, Armitage?'

'Stick insects,' I replied.

'Let's have a look, then,' he said.

I said, 'Best not to, they're sleeping.'

I think he was about to insist on a viewing but his mate on the back seat had just opened a packet of Capstan Full Strength and he was called away for a smoke, dragging his knuckles on the floor as he went. Not that the contents of the biscuit tin would always have been recognizable as food. Most weeks, no matter how much I followed the recipe or how many times I whipped the cream, I seemed to do nothing more than turn perfectly good ingredients into an inedible compost of unidentifiable biomass. And because Mum had forked out hard-earned housekeeping money on the ingredients, there was an expectation that whatever I'd produced at school in Tuesday afternoon's home economics class would form the basis of the Armitage family's evening meal later that day. On my return, Mum would prise open the tin lid like an Egyptologist opening some ancient casket, hoping to find treasure but more often than not discovering some dark, amorphous item in a partial state of decomposition. On one occasion I was so repulsed by the substance I'd produced – rissoles in tomato gravy, I think – that I poured the entire dishful down a manhole at the end of the street and told my mum it had been so delicious I hadn't been able to stop myself eating it on the way home.

Of course there's nothing wrong with being male and being a cook. In these more enlightened times it's probably a cool thing for guys to do, and even back then, it would have made sound political and practical sense for schoolboys to learn how to prepare a meal and wipe down a Formica work surface. But there was something about the seventies, something kind of Soviet about the gender divide, with the Berlin Wall still separating the sexes. At least that's how it felt to me, at my school, a cattle-market comprehensive of 1,800 kids and an uncountable number of unnameable teachers. On reflection, the staff did their very best, attempting to steer the optimum number of students towards moderate success, and the trick as a pupil was to be part of that broad and anonymous herd of children heading for some achievable and acceptable qualification at the far end of the canyon. The thing to avoid, therefore, at all costs, was attention. And if you *were* going to draw attention to yourself, there was a sliding scale of seriousness. In reverse order, stupidity was the least risky, leading to persistent but good-natured piss-taking. Followed by brilliance, which might attract bullying or at worst a beating. Followed by individuality, most heinous of all crimes, punishable by a life sentence of misery. Hence the terror of domestic science. But if cooking lessons themselves weren't sufficiently shaming and potentially damaging for a fourteen-year-old school-boy in semi-rural West Huddersfield, Colne Valley High School had come up with a master plan to elevate embar-rassment and humiliation to an all-time high. Many schools at that time had swimming pools, many had language labs. Some had art studios and some had music studios; some even had radio stations. But how many comprehensive schools in seventies Britain could boast the addition of a 'flat'? Not a schoolroom made to look like a room in a house where students might spend an afternoon learning life skills, but an actual penthouse apartment with decent carpets, pictures on the wall, its own little toilet with pink loo roll and matching rugs, and a balcony with panoramic views over the Pennine uplands. For students enrolled in domestic science, their week in the flat was seen as the highpoint of their course, the ultimate perk, during which they could wear their own clothes, make their own meals, and generally stand aloof from the timetable and rulebook. Which was terrific, if you were a girl. And would have been terrific for me as well if I'd been paired up with a girl; I could have spent a week in the company of some beautiful young woman who in the general order of things wouldn't have come anywhere near me. But I was with Mick. And Mick was with me. We had to put on our pinnies and we had to hoover and we had to dust. We had to iron curtains and polish horse brasses. In my warped memory, I remember us like Eric and Ernie, swanning around in dressing gowns and slippers, tapping the barometer and checking the oven to see if the soufflé had risen. There wasn't a bedroom, of course, and we didn't have to stay the night. But having kept our little secret for nearly eighteen months, we were now on full public display. We were four floors up, and directly opposite stood the glass-fronted B Block, like the wing of an open prison, which housed some of the school's most notorious and high-risk students. The first time we opened the French windows and stepped out on to the balcony, we might as well have been holding hands and announcing our engagement.

Pupils spending time in the flat were obliged to invite individual teachers for lunch; as well as putting our catering skills to the test we could practise the finer points of conversation and table manners. One particularly obnoxious teacher invited himself for a meal. I can't remember what we talked about, but the menu that day consisted largely of rissoles in tomato gravy. There was a little record player in the flat, and one record, which I swear was Max Bygraves singing 'The Deck of Cards'. I failed my domestic science course by neglecting to turn up for the written part of the exam and therefore receiving a grade X. I also made a complete hash of the practical, electing to produce a loaf of bread that was probably the only loaf in culinary history to actually reduce in size during baking, and steak flambé, which in the absence of a fire blanket was eventually put out of its misery with a wet tea towel. I wasn't proud of my grade X but think of it now with a certain amount of amusement. At least it wasn't as bad as the swathe of results reportedly achieved

by my mate's brother a few years later. This particular
student took four A levels. He failed three of them and
scraped an O level grade in the other. On the punched
strip of paper which confirmed the grades, the outside
column read F OFF.

*

How, I wonder, did celebrity chef Raymond Blanc sauté
and drizzle his way through the French education system?
What would *he* have served his geography teacher on a
wet Wednesday lunchtime? And is he in the kitchen
tonight as Speedy Sue and myself take a seat in his restaurant and one of his many minions drapes an ironed
linen napkin over my lap?

We've come to Le Manoir aux Quat' Saisons for a treat.
Speedy Sue came here once before, about fifteen years
ago, and remembered it as amazing and unbelievable and
a once-in-a-lifetime experience, and like most once-in-a-
lifetime experiences people tend to want to have them
again. So here we are. It was supposed to be a surprise,
but it isn't, because I'd punched the postcode into the
satellite navigation system (her surprise present to me),
and we'd only driven about ten yards when it politely
announced the name of our destination. What *is* a surprise
to my wife, however, is the recalibrated date of our
wedding anniversary. A couple of months ago, when I
phoned, the lady taking the booking asked if we were
celebrating a special occasion. And because I was still
choking on the price she'd just quoted for one night's
accommodation, I blurted out that we were. After all, at
the Sole Mio in Huddersfield if you tell them it's your
birthday they bring you a banana with a glacé cherry on

le **Manoir**
AUX QUAT' SAISONS

Good Morning

Today's weather forecast
Date: 21/01/07

am —————————— pm

Temperature 8 °C 46 °F

the end and two dollops of anatomically positioned ice cream. For free. I must have been thinking that a bunch of red roses in the room or a bottle of Moët in a bucket of ice would soften the blow. But obviously I hadn't been thinking hard enough, because I hadn't anticipated the receptionist, who greets us personally at the door on our arrival, saying, 'And may I ask, is it a significant number?'

'Only to us,' I mumble. I've no idea what I mean by this remark but he seems to be satisfied with the answer. In a quiet corner of the lobby a few minutes later, I confess to Speedy Sue that not only are we outside our comfort zone both financially and culturally, but we're obliged to pretend that our marriage took place on this very date, and that for the sake of my credibility, this deception must persist for the duration of our visit. In other words, I'm a skinflint and a liar.

There's nothing to do here except spend money and eat, usually simultaneously, although I notice from the brochure that a clay pigeon shoot could have been arranged, and that we could have availed ourselves of the helicopter landing pad, had I the foresight to have pre-booked. The literature in the room encourages us to take a walk around the organic vegetable garden. Maybe in summer it's a visual and olfactory orgy of naturally grown produce. And maybe in the depth of an old-fashioned winter, when manicured shrubs are seized by frost, the scene becomes one of brittle and crystallized beauty. But on a globally warmed Saturday at the end of January we could be stumbling around a retired miner's allotment in a backwater of Rotherham. A couple of cabbages are making the effort, and the odd clump of broccoli perhaps, but not much else. Like us, other couples, inappropriately dressed for a turn around a walled field, are picking their way along the muddy paths, poking at things with their fashionable shoes and looking for something to comment on. In the Japanese Garden I stand inside a bamboo-clad hut waiting for a Zen moment or for a koi carp to ghost silently through my consciousness, but nothing happens. The wooden bridge is cordoned off for safety reasons. The ornamental pond is stagnant and full of twigs. There are several pieces of naff statuary, including a life-size scarecrow (in as much as a scarecrow can have a life) with a blackbird on his arm. We go next door to look at the church, which is locked, then we walk into the village of Great Milton, which is very pretty but also closed, then we go back to the room and fill the enormous bath with bubbles.

We're in the Dovecote. It's two circular rooms, like two hatboxes one on top of the other. Downstairs it's a luxury bathroom and office combined, always handy for emailing a few spreadsheets during a power shower or receiving an international business call without having to vacate the toilet. Upstairs it's mainly a bed. A very big bed and a very soft bed, and behind it – the thing I'd been most looking forward to clapping my eyes on – the 'enhanced LED headboard'. Depicted in the online brochure as some kind of portal into the next universe, in real life it's more like a pub-size plasma screen TV with Christmas lights embedded within it. Being Saturday, I think it might be able to receive my favourite programme (*Soccer Saturday*, anchored by Jeff Stelling, in which a panel of football experts talk excitedly about the live matches they're not allowed to show; what Speedy Sue calls 'radio on the telly') but when I aim the remote control at it there's a whirring and clunking noise from somewhere behind me and the actual telly is thrust upwards from within a wooden cabinet. It's not a new telly. In fact it's a bit knackered, and it doesn't get Sky Sports, so with a whirr and a clunk, down it goes.

Lying on the bed, the eye is drawn to the roof of the Dovecote, which is worthy of mention. There's no ceiling, just exposed original beams radiating from a central strut reinforced by a metal brace. Drapes flow downwards and outwards to give the impression of a teepee or Arabian tent. The roof then funnels away to a circular chimney at the very top, in which there seems to be a mirror and several windows. And not until next morning does it occurs to us that either by accident or design the mirrored turret, like some kind of reverse camera obscura, might be capable of optically relaying images from within the sumptuous boudoir to all quarters of Le Manoir.

The lounge in the main house is all fireplaces and settees. The people who come here a lot talk loudly and confidently. The people who've never been before look as if they're waiting to see a consultant, and speak in whispers. We scan the wine list, which ranges from about fifteen quid to over a thousand, and go for the second least expensive. There are three menus to choose from, and not a rissole in sight. Unfortunately, two people can't choose from separate menus because they contain different numbers of courses, and this would lead to problems of timing, which even at £95 a head cannot possibly be resolved. We go for five courses, and are seated next to a sweet couple in their late sixties who have opted for what in a lesser eating emporium might be described as 'the works'. At one point I look across and see that they have been served what is, in anyone's language, a boiled egg. All the other couples in the restaurant seem to be made up of small youngish men with older largish women, and I wonder if we've arrived here on the one night of the year when Oxfordshire jockeys take their aunties out for a meal. Some of the food is delicious, such as the squab, which is pigeon, right? (My friend Mark later points out that we'd probably been served pigeon because we were staying in the Dovecote, and on that basis should be grateful we weren't staying in the old stables.) And some of it is a bit daft, such as the haddock and whisky soup, which is haddock soup with whisky in it, right? But the true daftness is reserved for the pudding. In fact the *Nature morte hivernale* is less like a dessert and more like the set design for a children's television programme, with meringue toadstools and other fairy-tale features sculpted from various sugary confections. We look longingly at the cheeseboard that passes between other diners but is not part of our chosen itinerary. No doubt if we opened our mouths the staff here would be only too pleased to accommodate our preference. But we're not like that. It's not in our nature. Besides which, we're pretending to be celebrating our wedding anniversary, and in an environment like this where falsehoods seem to be magnified tenfold, we might as well be having an affair. After the meal there's not much to do except listen to a man with a Manhattan/Brummie accent talk about golf courses on the Algarve, so we retire to the Dovecote and fill the bath again. There's a sound system in the room. Not the latest Bang & Olufsen as you might have expected, but a mid-price Denon with a scratched facia. With little or no radio reception, I fish around in the drawer underneath

29

and find the following CDs: *Ultimate Classics, the Essential Masterpieces*; *Robbie Williams – Greatest Hits*; and something by Bob Hope. When it comes to music, I've always been a fascist, prepared to make an instant judgement on someone's character with nothing more than a cursory glance at their record collection. And whether these are CDs provided by the management to suit the taste of their clientele or CDs left in the room by previous inhabitants, it amounts to the same thing. Before we leave the next morning, I fetch a copy of *Colossal Youth* from the car, the one and only album by the one and only Young Marble Giants, and leave it in the drawer beneath the stereo, for the benefit of future guests and their aural pleasure. There isn't a charge for this service; I do it gladly, of my own free will, and at my own expense.*

It would be highly indiscreet and not a little churlish to say how much bed, breakfast and evening meal in the bosom of the English countryside sets us back, but including the deposit and not including a tip, let me say that out of £946.15, there is very little change.

* I can strongly recommend this form of reverse shoplifting; as a practice it offers all the adrenalin rush of actual theft with few of the risks, plus the participant gets to bask in the warm afterglow of philanthropic altruism. In 1992 I committed a more egotistical version of the same crime in City Lights bookshop in San Francisco. On the day I visited, it seemed as if every wall of that bookstore was crammed to the ceiling with slim volumes by poets from every corner of the globe, with one disappointing omission. The next day I went back, surreptitiously pulled a copy of my first book, *Zoom!*, from under my jacket, and slipped it into the shelf between Edwin Arlington Robinson and Matthew Arnold. And for all I know, there it still sits, passed over by browsers and stocktakers, but proud to be occupying a compressed centimetre or so of prized poetic real estate.

Stiff Little Fingers
Holmfirth Picturedrome
4 October 2004

I went with my mate Jock to see the Jam in Leeds. It must have been 1980 – we were still at school. Wanting to look the part, we'd rummaged around in the under-stage wardrobe of the village am-dram society, and went to the gig dressed in military service uniform. Like the 'Little Boy Soldiers' from the *Setting Sons* album they were touring at the time, we must have looked like Wilfred Owen and Siegfried Sassoon preparing to go over the top. The venue was an enormous tram shed of a place, still reeking of beer from the real ale festival preceding the gig, but even with just two guitars and a set of drums the band filled it with noise. They were incredibly sharp – the music seemed to be made of ricochets and reflections. I dived in and lost my dog tag in the mayhem. We knew we wouldn't make the last train home, so on the basis that a good lie is a whopping big lie we'd invented a Polish friend who lived in Headingley and told our parents we were staying at his place for the night. We'd even given him a name, Pavel; Mum and Dad would have been justified in wondering how two village boys from the Pennine foothills were suddenly best mates with an Eastern European émigré living on the far side of metropolitan West Yorkshire, but thankfully they never asked.

Which was just as well, because the details of our lie didn't extend that far. It fizzled out somewhere around Mirfield or Dewsbury. After the gig we found a twenty-four-hour cafe at the top end of the city centre. The owner, sensing we were new to this game and there for the night, explained that there were only three rules. First, we weren't allowed to go to sleep. Second, we had to buy something at least once an hour. And third, no drugs. Being the seventeen-year-old son of a probation officer born and brought up on the edge of the moors, rule three didn't present much of a problem. At that stage, a bottle of cider from the offy or a flagon of home-brewed damson wine usually did the trick. And rule one was counteracted by rule two, the obligatory hourly intake of sheep-dip-coloured tea or treacly tasting coffee producing just enough of a caffeine surge to suppress the growing tiredness for a further sixty minutes. Also, the fear and excitement acted as a stimulant. All through the night, exotic-looking people entered the establishment. In our alcove under the stairs we were like tourists on safari, crouched in a hide, watching the big game visiting the watering hole. With their Mohicans and piercings these extraordinary creatures strutted and preened. On their T-shirts they wore the names of bands I'd read about but never heard. They occupied the window seats or the middle tables, talking loudly about records and gigs. They openly violated rule three. One utterly unselfconscious and savagely beautiful lad with peroxide hair and a studded dog collar drummed on the Formica with his fists and barked out a song called 'Where Were You?' Most were not much older than me and quite a few were a couple of years younger, but in terms of coolness and credibility they were light years ahead – from another planet. By the time I found out that 'Where Were You?' was a single by the Mekons, it was already three years old and out of stock. I don't think the blond boy in the all-night cafe looked in our direction or even noticed us as we cupped our mugs of char and blended into the wallpaper, but in my own mind, his chanted taunt was being performed directly for my benefit.

I'm telling this story to a couple of friends in a pub called the Nook, the memory having been triggered by the name Bruce Foxton, now playing bass with Belfast punk veterans Stiff Little Fingers. Stiff Little Fingers: Jake Burns still shouting about an alternative Ulster and suspect devices twenty years on. Stiff Little Fingers, with Bruce Foxton on bass, about to play Holmfirth Picturedrome in ten minutes' time. We sup up and wander across the road, leaving the health food outlet Your Nuts to our left and Sid's 'Last of the Summer Wine' Cafe to our right, a combination which tells you pretty much everything you need to know about the locality. As we walk into the shadowy, beery venue and see the silhouettes of a few hundred skinheads, I think there's going to be trouble. But once my eyes have adjusted to the darkness I realize they aren't skinheads at all. They're just bald.

For as long as the Nook has been known as the Nook, its actual title, as a licensed establishment, was the Rose and Crown. Finally, however, in what was generally seen as a triumph of the popular voice over the forces of bureaucracy, the Rose and Crown sign was taken down and a sign saying 'The Nook' was put up. At which point some locals said it had 'sold out'. It's not that easy to find, being situated in a kind of mugger's alley, protected by a buffer zone of cafes and bistros, but the determined drinker will usually arrive there eventually. In the early eighties, as well as selling good beer, the bar staff were none too inquisitive about the precise age of some of the younger customers, and as long as you took off your school blazer and tie, a drink was almost guaranteed. The Nook had the best jukebox this side of Huddersfield, including 'Teenage Kicks' and Talking Heads' 'Psycho Killer', at a time when most other pubs were offering sloppy ballads or lorry-driving heavy metal, with very little in between. The walls of the back room – an extension at the side of the river – had been plastered but never painted, presenting an irresistible canvas for talented graffiti artists and smart-alec would-be poets. The first time I heard the Damned's 'New Rose' was in the Nook: 'Is she really going out with him?' followed by cardboard-box drums, all-thumbs guitaring, then that superb, shouted syllable – not 'oi', or 'huh', or God forbid 'hey', but a kind of stabbed-in-the-stomach 'ah' that becomes an even more painful utterance when reprised a minute or so later.

The Nook was a half-hour bus ride from Marsden, and a two-hour walk home if you'd invested your bus fare in alcoholic beverages and independent music. My local pub was the Shakespeare, but they played Saxon and were not keen on sixth-formers popping in for a pint after school. Like every other son and daughter of the Colne Valley, on the morning of my eighteenth birthday I received a letter on House of Commons stationery from our MP, the Right Honourable Richard Wainwright. Presumably he was looking forward to my support in the next election, now I was eligible to vote. Clutching the letter as proof of age, I walked proudly into the Shakespeare, laid it out on the bar and requested a pint of bitter. Without even speaking, the hairy-armed landlord served me with a glass of Coke and a bag of crisps then returned to his conversation with three or four oily mechanics at the far end of the bar. Cheers.

On the Road 1

I am met off the train by an extremely nervous woman in a hire car who is generating a thermonuclear amount of heat and cannot locate the demist function on the console. In a cloud of condensation we drive to a local cafe where she restricts my choice of meal according to her authorized budget. I have forgotten to bring any books. I visit the local bookshop to purchase a copy of my *Selected Poems* and am recognized by the man at the till. He says nothing, but his expression is one of pathos.

The venue is a Portakabin in a car park. The PA system is a Fisher-Price karaoke machine. I am introduced as 'The name on everyone's lips: Simon Armriding'. A well-intentioned youth doing voluntary work for the aurally challenged (of which there are none in the audience) has offered to 'sign'. He stands to my left all evening, giving what is a passable impersonation of Ian Curtis dancing to 'She's Lost Control', and eventually keels over. Five minutes before the interval, a nice lady from the WI goes into the kitchenette at the back to begin tea-making operations. My final poem of the half is accompanied by the organ-like hum of a wall-mounted water heater rising slowly towards boiling point. There is no alcohol but how about a cup of Bovril? Following the break, an old man at the front falls asleep and farts during a poem about death / suffering / self-pity etc. Afterwards, there are no books for

sale but some kind soul asks me to autograph her copy of
Summoned by Bells.

My designated driver, the radioactive woman, trans-
ports me in her mobile sauna to an Indian restaurant on
the high street. She is allergic to curry (for fear of meltdown, presumably) but waits for me in the car while I
guzzle a meal of not more than £5 in value (including
drinks) paid for by food voucher. I am staying with old
Mr Farter in the suburbs. He has gone home to give the
Z-bed an airing and to prepare a selection of his poems
for my perusal, the first of which, 'The Mallard', begins
'Thou, oh monarch of the riverbank'. I 'sleep' fully clothed
on a pube-infested sheet next to an asthmatic Border
collie. Ungraciously and with great stealth I leave the
house before dawn and wander through empty, un-
familiar avenues heading vaguely towards the tallest buildings on the skyline. It is three hours before the first train
home. I breakfast with winos and junkies in McDonald's.
Killing time in the precinct, I find a copy of one of my
early volumes in a dump-bin on the pavement outside the
charity shop. The price is ten pence. It is a signed copy.
Under the signature, in my own handwriting, are the
words 'To Mum and Dad'.

On the (Rail) Road

I'm not a stamp collector, I'm not a railway enthusiast, I need eight hours' sleep a night and my drink of choice after six o'clock in the evening is wine or beer. So why am I knocking on the steel gates of the Royal Mail Distribution Centre in a dark and frightening part of London at 11 p.m. with a teacup in my hand, about to board a train? The unlikely answer to that question is this: I'm a poet. Almost seventy years ago, another poet, W. H. Auden, wrote the poem 'Night Mail' about the Travelling Post Office. It began

> This is the Night Mail crossing the Border,
> Bringing the cheque and the postal order,

lines which have gone down in history. Unfortunately, the TPO is about to go the same way. The rail service that for well over 150 years has sorted and delivered mail to the far-flung corners of Britain is to be phased out, replaced by big red transporter wagons and their clod-hopping carbon footprints, and whereas Auden was employed to celebrate the TPO, I am here to commemorate it.

My visit begins in not untypical fashion, i.e. explaining as clearly as possible the details of my improbable mission, then waiting at a counter while the man on the other side of the glass picks up a telephone and says something like 'There's this poet in reception' or 'You're not going to believe this, but . . .' Through the toughened glass in the fire exit, I watch a rat amble across the car park, not in the least bit hurried by the glare of the security lights or the rumble of articulated lorries. Then eventually someone has heard of me, or remembers me, and I'm shown upstairs to a balcony overlooking the sorting area. In an orthodox railway station the place below me would be described as the concourse and would be filled with milling passengers and the distorted echo of departure announcements. But here the whole space is taken up by one enormous Heath-Robinson-style contraption made of wheels and motors. At the far end, the 'goods in' part of the building, a mudslide of mainly Manila-coloured envelopes and parcels is being poured into the giant machine. The contents are then ferried upwards and inwards, then onwards through what seems to be a kind of intestinal network of tubes and ducts. And somewhere within that huge contrivance, by a process possibly known only to God or the wizard who created it, each individual package and letter is 'sorted', and emerges through a mouthpiece at the very top, before being tipped on to a smooth-running conveyor belt and deposited into one of several dozen trolleys or sacks at the bottom of several dozen spiral chutes. The whole apparatus might have come directly from Willy Wonka's Chocolate Factory. I wouldn't mind a ride on it myself. At the 'goods out' end, the sorted mail is trundled towards a series of vast portals, and through the swinging strips of dirty plastic curtaining I catch an occasional glimpse of a train. In a perfect testament to the Great British Workforce, nine tenths of the people on the shop floor beneath me are working like stink, and the other 10 per cent are reading the early edition of the *Daily Mirror*. In a pile of mail in a three-sided cage on the far side of the hall, one man appears to be asleep.

On the platform I decide it's time to talk to someone.

'Can I ask you your name?'

'Bob.'

'How long have you been working on these trains, Bob?'

'Fifteen years.'

'And what are you going to be doing tomorrow?'

'Fuck all, mate.'

He's standing by a trestle table covered by a white tablecloth, with several dishes on offer including chicken goujons and well-sculpted melon balls. I ask Bob if it's normal working practice for the Post Office to lay on a finger buffet before the trains set off into the night.

'No, mate,' he replies. 'Last supper.'

Gallows humour, it appears, will be the preferred method of communication from this point on.

Auden saw himself as a poet who could turn his hand to any kind of verse, whether it be the most intricate formal sequence intended for a literary publication or a casual rhyme for a friend's birthday. I'm of a similar mind, holding the view that any situation or scene can be expressed as poetry, though on first inspection the train itself isn't very inspiring. Inside it's a bit grubby: the walls are painted prison grey or hospital blue, and have suffered the bumps and bruises of a million mail sacks and sharp-pointed packages. And it's empty – no seats, just work-benches and sorting stations. And it's cold. And it's gloomy – the windows are nothing more than grimed-up port-holes. So with no point of reference on the outside I haven't really noticed that we've set off. But it's kind of exciting, in a *Boy's Own* sort of way. In fact the whole environment is very male indeed. Rumours circulate of the men on these trains living two lives: a life at home as a husband and father, then a second life at the far end of the line, in Newcastle or Carlisle or Plymouth, a life of public houses, licensed betting offices, golf courses and long-term lovers. The life of Riley, we might call it. Without actually using the word bigamy, I ask Jim, nine-teen years on these trains, if any of the rumours are actually true. 'No,' he says. Then a huge smile opens up across his face, and he adds, 'But if you are going to get up to that kind of thing, I suppose three hundred miles away from home is as good a place as any.' Then he says something else but I can't hear him under the noise of the train, which is suddenly swaying and shaking and rattling along and apparently going very fast indeed. The noise is painful, but no one seems to bother.

'What speed are we doing?' I shout at him.

''Bout a hundred, maybe,' he mouths back.

To look down the length of the train is to stare along a never-ending corridor, where men (they are all men) in Post Office overalls lug huge bags of mail from one carriage to another, or deal vast piles of letters into various slots and pigeonholes, or scoop parcels and packets out of deep troughs and shunt them into sacks. There isn't a buffet car, hence the instruction to bring my own cup, and the rust-coloured tea from the ancient-looking urn tastes as if it's been stewing since the day the train was built. Everything about the whole experience, in fact, has a historical feel to it, and puts me in mind of an age before mass communication. Before email and fax, even before the telephone. The age of the love letter, when promises of the heart were carried on trains like this, and arrived before breakfast. A world I never really knew. When the noise subsides for a minute or so, Jim tells me he's going to doss around for a few weeks, maybe dip into his redundancy package and take a holiday or even a cruise, then look for a new job. Ideally, he'd like to drive unregistered vehicles to car dealerships all over the country. It's like listening to some institutionalized old lag, too set in his ways now to simply go home and settle down. All he wants is the journey, never the destination, and if it can't be on the old iron horse then it'll have to be in a brand new car. I say to him, 'So you'll be one of those blokes thumbing a lift on the slip road with a red number plate in one hand and a cardboard sign saying "Brent Cross" in the other, will you?'

'That'll be me,' he says, kind of dreamily.

I set off down the train in search of Dino, who I'm told was on the very TPO held up at Bridego railway bridge by Ronnie Biggs and his gang back in 1963. I figure that Dino will either be some square-jawed man with a steely glint in his eye capable of repelling would-be robbers, or some damaged and possibly doolally individual with a hammer dent in his head. But Dino is an even-tempered old-timer with a small voice and a disappointing tendency towards honesty. So even though I make it perfectly clear that I'm prepared to believe any lie he wants to tell me, he prefers to stick to the truth and the facts, and says that although the incident did indeed take place on this line, his train was travelling in the opposite direction. Which isn't the story I wanted to hear.

'Maybe you're just saying that because Ronnie put the frighteners on you,' I say, offering him the opportunity of dramatic hyperbole.

'No, it was definitely going the other way,' says Dino flatly.

Forty-odd years later trains still go 'the other way'. He's referring to the fact that just as 100 Londoners and 30,000 items of mail are heading north during the night, a similar train performing the same operation is heading south carrying letters to the capital, full of Geordies or Scotsmen. The two teams never actually meet but pass each other at some indeterminate point in the darkness at a combined speed of 200 miles an hour.

'I suppose you all stick your backsides out of the window when you go past,' I say, trying to find a weakness in Dino's defences.

Dino says no, they don't do that. Then he says, 'By the way, I'm not called Dino. My name's Geoff.'

The TPO is heading further north, but I jump off at York. I'm looking for a proper train to go home on. One with seats and a conductor. Or more probably a taxi. It's two in the morning, I've got a few notes in my notebook, a ringing deafness in both ears, and a teacup in my hand.

*

Poets tend to look for coincidence and synchronicity, even when it doesn't exist. So as a poet I'm tempted to think that the indeterminate point on the east coast line somewhere between London and Newcastle might well be the same location from where I'm dialling 999 about a month later.

The woman's voice says, 'Where are you, exactly?' It's a question put to me by a switchboard operator from South Yorkshire Fire Service as I peer through the window of a train into the black night beyond. I've been on the train for four hours, the last two spent in silence, coldness and complete darkness, ever since a loud bang and a shower of sparks brought it to a slow, gliding halt. There is a smell of smoke. The woman on the phone is trying to pinpoint our precise location.

> Her: What can you see?
> Me: Nothing. It's dark.
> Her: Nothing at all? Any landmarks?
> Me: A tree.
> (*Pause*)
> Her: Hmm. You see, our maps aren't really that detailed.

I'm not alone in the compartment. At the next table are four Yorkshire businessmen just returned from a trip to China. They've been talking loudly and drinking lager. Whether I'm interested or not, by Grantham there isn't much I don't know about construction opportunities in Guangdong Province or which hotels in Nanjing have the softest bathrobes. There's a city in the east which is bigger than London and makes nothing but zips and press-studs, apparently. However, during the past hour their thoughts have turned away from investment portfolios in the Pacific Rim and moved towards our immediate predicament. Like a team of executives on a television challenge show, they have formed something of an escape committee, the main task being to prise open the sliding door and make contact with the next carriage. But even fuelled by premium-strength continental lager their efforts are in vain. The doors, the intercom, the lights, in fact anything powered by electricity, has ceased to function, as has the air conditioning, reminding us that the human being when trapped in a confined space is a stinking animal, and that the toilets of trains, when not served by ventilation, are malodorous places. The gang of four have also delegated responsibility to other passengers. One man has taken possession of the metal toffee-hammer located above the luggage rack and is trying to recall a Radio 4 feature he once heard about weak spots in the windows of trains. Another man is scrambling around under the seats looking for a trapdoor. All this happens in silhouette. Everyone is taking it in turns to use their mobile phone as a torch, everyone except me. Remember Hatfield? Remember Paddington? Remember the astonishingly named Great Heck? My assigned task is to use what power remains in my mobile to make an actual call and to let someone know where we are before the next GNER service north hammers into us at 125 mph and we are atomized into non-existence. This is a particular concern for the occupants of our carriage, carriage T, which forms the rear of the train. Eventually the switchboard operator calls back.

'Are you the gentleman that phoned the fire brigade?'

'Yes.'

'There's no need to worry. Some kids have thrown a shopping trolley on to the overhead cables. Just for the logbook, can you give me your name?'

I tell her my name.

She says, 'Are you that poetry person?'

I say that I am.

She says, 'How funny – my daughter did you for her exams.'

I tell her that's a nice coincidence.

She says, 'Not really. She failed.'

The Last Post

Love these days is the blink of an eye:
mile-high love in an aeroplane,
lay-by love at the end of a lane,
satellite love in the radio-waves,

      but ours was written, ours was signed,
      we were lovers all through the night,
      lovers by watermark, lovers by mail,
      we were lovers by morning light,
      we were lovers by rail.

Words as pixels, words as bytes,
word of mouth at the speed of light –
the world these days is the world on a plate,
love these days is easily sent,
but ours was longhand, ours was meant,

      our love vowed to arrive by breakfast,
      dealt on the table, leant on the tea-pot,
      propped on the butter-dish, slotted in the toast-rack,
      our love lived by the stamp and the post-mark.

Ours was sifted and sorted and tagged,
bundled and counted and numbered and bagged
by men with dimpled rubber thumbs,

by men with ink instead of blood,
by men with rubber bands for wrists,
with postal-codes for fingerprints,

    in a train with a letterbox cut in its side,
    by bin-men and corner-men working the ride,
    in the juddering, stammering mine of mail,
    in the lumbering, cantering vein of mail,
    in the rumbling, clattering seam of mail,
    in the thundering, hammering aisle of mail.

      Up to the capital, down to the north,
      our love passed on the opposite track,
      our love curved through shunting yards,
      our love climbed the Devon Bank,
      our love moved while the nation slept,
      our love crossed in the graveyard shift,
      our love swayed by the phase of the moon,
      our love woke the nightingale,
      turned the head of the tawny owl.

        Love by the arc of the constellations,
        love like special operations,
        love like a signal, love like a rumour,
        undercover love like a military manoeuvre.

Letters to last, letters for life,
sealed by tongue and opened by knife.
Life these days is a world away.
Love these days is an after-word,

49

but ours was written, ours was signed,
we were lovers all through the night,
lovers by watermark, lovers by mail,
we were lovers by morning light,
we were lovers by rail.

Mile after mile after mile after mile
we were lovers by rail.

Songbirds

When I jacked in my career as a probation officer in the mid-nineties to become a full-time poet, it never occurred to me that I'd end up writing for television. In those days, I probably held the lofty, moral position that poetry and television were complete opposites, and that verse could only be devalued by the small screen. I've changed my tune since then; poetry, I think, is a vital, life-affirming substance, and can operate right across the media, not just between the covers of a book. When I received my P45 from the Home Office, I also imagined that I'd never have to set foot in a prison again, unless something went badly awry. Turns out I got that wrong as well.

Songbirds is the seventh film I've made with Brian Hill at Century Films. The first time he called me, about ten years ago, he wanted to know if I could provide a poetic commentary for a film he was making called *Saturday Night*. Despite the London dialling code, I could hear Lancastrian vowels in his accent, so on a very crude level I anticipated we'd have something to talk about, even if it was only the M62. Brian once lived on the infamous Ashfield Valley estate, the brutalist system-built housing project on the outskirts of Rochdale that was thought of by many as a kind of thieves' playground. As a fresh-faced probation officer I often tramped along its sky-terraces, its concrete walkways and connecting bridges, usually looking over my shoulder, and it's interesting to think that if Brian had decided to make his living by selling smack through his letter box rather than setting up his own production company, he might have been a name on my caseload rather than a speed-dial on my mobile.

Songbirds is set in Downview Prison in Surrey, and it's a follow-up to *Feltham Sings*, a film we made in Feltham Young Offenders' Institution, the notorious bad boys' nick not far from Heathrow. As well as being documentaries, both films are also 'musicals'. Inmates talk about their experiences of offending and prison life, then suddenly burst into song. The difference is that Downview is a women's prison. So instead of tenor and bass voices, this time we hear soprano and contralto. And instead of testosterone-driven rap about gang violence and car-jackings, this time we hear more sorrowful tunes. There are some desperately sad women in Downview and so there are some sad moments in the film. There are also uplifting and hilarious ones. In a building known as Contract Services, selected inmates can earn a few quid a day by untangling writhing black knots of aeroplane headphones and repacking them in individual plastic bags. In *Songbirds*, this factory floor becomes the setting for the 'Drug Mule Chorus' – a dozen women swaying and singing among the wires and workbenches, while the prison wardens watch through the glass, tapping their toes.

My role in these projects is as a songwriter. I went to Downview, strolled around the gardens and the wings, chatted with the inmates and tried to identify the birds of prey. No one ever explained the presence of several buzzards and other large raptors tethered outside one of the blocks, just as no one had ever explained the presence of several peacocks strutting around on the roofs of Feltham, or why the radiating wings of that prison were named after ducks and waders. In these days of sponsorship and endorsement, perhaps the British penal system has come to some sort of happy arrangement with the RSPB, or maybe the governors of those two institutions are trying to make a metaphorical point by surrounding their inmates with flightless and shackled beasts. After visiting the nick just once, I then sat at home, 200 miles away, with a minidisc player in one hand and a pen in the other, listening to the spoken testimonies of several prisoners and trying to turn them into lyrics. I could have spent more time in the prison, but I don't think it would have helped. I'm the sort of writer who needs distance and dispassion to be able to tackle a subject. For me, writing is like dissecting a rat – something done with a clinical eye under laboratory-type conditions. To get more involved on a personal level might have meant donning my probation officer's hat again, when the poet's one has become so comfortable. I've already given up the job once – I don't want to go back.

Another difference between this film and the last is the amount of sympathy I feel for the prisoners. True, some of Downview's female population have done some utterly terrible things, but there's no escaping the fact that the majority of women in the prison are victims. There's barely a single inmate who hasn't been abused in one way or another. Like the woman who was sexually assaulted with a weightlifting bar. Like the woman who was raped with a revolver. Like the woman whose husband gave her regular black eyes to remind her that she belonged to him. Lurking in the background of each of these stories is a violent partner, a monstrous father, a desperate junkie, a heartless dealer, a sleazy pimp . . . some bastard, always a man. My head tells me it doesn't excuse the crime; my heart says that it probably does.

When the lyrics are complete they're passed on to the composer Simon Boswell, who must be some kind of genius because a few days later they come back and they're songs. The next stage is to show each song to the prisoner whose words inspired it. To give them *their song*. I'm not present when this handover takes place, but I'm told it produces some surprising reactions, one of which is gratitude. It must be strange to be confronted with a ballad or R & B number, the lyrics of which are a detailed description of your own crack habit or a verse-by-verse account of the night you set fire to your husband. But rather than be embarrassed or defensive, most of the women are simply flabbergasted that someone should take the time and trouble to tell their side of the story. Throughout their lives, most women who end up behind bars have had things taken from them, most notably their dignity.

The films I've made with Brian aren't conventional by any means. On paper, asking documentary characters to sing and dance might sound exploitative, or a bit of a freak show. But our motives are clear. First, we want to make films that are meaningful and memorable. Second, all documentaries are 'authored' in some way – we're just being upfront about it. And third, although we don't see ourselves as social workers of the television schedules, the subjects in our films are often people without a voice. Prisoners, addicts, prostitutes, illegal immigrants – they all have something to say, and what we try to do is strengthen their voice. It's a form of empowerment, I'd argue, and as such no one does anything they don't want to. We spent months working with one inmate in Downview – let's call her G – and finally produced a gospel song for her. She wanted to sing about her offence (drug importation) in the context of her Christian beliefs. And we wanted her to sing the song in the prison chapel, in front of a stained-glass window, with coloured sunlight streaming through the air. She had a beautiful voice and she would have made a spectacular contribution to the film. On the day, though, she walked away. She didn't say why but she had her reasons; it was her business and no one else's. And she remained silent.

I sometimes wonder if the women in Downview will remember their songs. Ten years from now many of them will still be serving their sentences – but will they still be humming their tunes in their cells, or mouthing the lyrics as they tackle the millionth set of aeroplane headphones? Maggie becomes one of the central characters in *Songbirds*. Since being sent down, she's had to 'give up' all three of her children for adoption. She'll never see them again. So to say goodnight or goodbye to them, she asked me to write a lullaby, based on her own words and feelings. In a former life, Maggie was a singer in a bar. She has an instinctive feel for music and an astonishing voice that oscillates between Dublin and Nashville, Tennessee. She tells me she wants to croon her lullaby through the bars of her cell window, sending her words up into the darkening sky over south London, hoping that they find their mark.

The idea of putting songs into a documentary came by accident really, when one of the characters in an earlier film, *Drinking for England*, finally revealed himself to be the third and more wayward brother of the brothers Campbell of UB40 fame. But rather than use his throat as a conduit for song, brother Duncan had elected to use it as a siphoning device for alcoholic liquids, and had pissed half his life away in the urinals of Birmingham's public houses. We caught up with him on his fortieth birthday in one of his favoured watering holes. 'Here I am, bankrupt and potless,' he tells the camera between gulps of bitter and long drags on a ciggie, and goes on to describe how his life has conformed to the George Best school of thinking, namely that he has spent most of his income on booze, fags, gambling and loose women, and squandered the rest. I write a song for him called 'Thinking and Joking' (drinking and smoking – geddit?) and in my opinion he sings it with great confidence and no little talent. His pop star brothers are less impressed. Surrounded by an entourage of gofers and caddies, they turn up in absurd pop star clothes and make facetious remarks about the song I've written. 'It's crap,' one of them opines. And if crap means it won't be getting covered in thirty years' time by a white reggae band with Brummie accents and piped into shoe shops and supermarkets across the nation, then I'm happy to agree.

After *Drinking for England* we get more ambitious. Instead of just one character in the film singing a song, why don't they all sing? This leads us to Feltham YOI and eventually to HMP Downview, but sitting between them like a pork sausage between two slices of prison bread comes the small matter of *Pornography: The Musical*. When Brian suggested we make a film about women working in the sex industry, I was a little bit nervous. When it was panned on *Newsnight Review* I didn't hear the gist of the criticism because I was hiding behind the settee, and had just emerged on the night it was broadcast only to hear Channel 4 trailing it as the most sexually explicit film ever to be shown on national television. And clearly the considered opinions of Mark Kermode and Bonnie Greer fell on deaf ears because viewing figures were very healthy indeed. Unhealthily healthy, in fact, though whether the nation watched it as I did – through my fingers – is not recorded by market research.

Pornography: The Musical is really Kelly's story. She's been appearing in pornographic films for about a decade and is trying to get out of the game. She says the effects are disfiguring – both mentally and physically – and after watching her emerge from a bedroom dripping with urine, then listening to her describe what went on behind the door, it's not difficult to believe. Kelly, though, is the only dissenting voice we can find. All the other women we talk to are happy with their lot, and see what they do as both lucrative and glamorous. Even Rebecca who strips in a shabby pub in High Wycombe on a Thursday lunch-time, then tours the bar with a pint pot into which disinterested punters drop ten-pence pieces and the odd pound coin. Even the woman who is presenting a new line in sex toys, not in a film studio but on a length of decking in the garden of a modest semi-detached near Bristol. On a chilly spring morning we follow her and her production team (her 'director' and some bloke with a camcorder) out into the garden in her skimpy leatherette basque and pants. The device she is demonstrating is a two-pronged, angry-looking affair that reminds me of a space gun I once got in a boy's comic when I was nine or ten. The bloke with the camera zooms in and out while next door's dog comes and sits on the lawn and chews absent-mindedly on a rubber bone. It doesn't seem like the high life to me, but later, back in the house, as she rinses the offending object under the kitchen tap, she assures us she is living the dream.

But the central scene in the film belongs to porn star Faye Rampton and involves an activity I had never previously heard of and have not heard of since. The practice of Bukkake, she tells us, is derived from an ancient Japanese custom for dealing with unfaithful wives, in which the errant spouse is taken to a field on the outskirts of the village and buried up to her neck in sand. With no means of escape or evasion she must then accept her punishment and humiliation, provided by the men of the village, who gather above her and ejaculate on to her head. In truth, I haven't been able to discover if this is an actual cultural activity practised by ancient societies or simply a convenient story cooked up by the makers of dodgy films to give their work a kind of anthropological veracity. Either way, the word Bukkake seems to have entered the language of pornography, and film-makers in the industry are busily re-enacting it at a hotel near you. Seriously, next time you're in the Travelodge tearing open your sachet of instant coffee and peeling back the foil lid on a thimbleful of long-life milk, consider for a moment what might be happening just a few feet away on the other side of the partition wall.

Faye is adamant that she is a sex maniac, so for her Bukkake is a way of satisfying all her desires and getting paid at the same time. Here's how it works. In one room Faye dresses up in a blue and white PVC nurse's uniform and lies down on the bed, ready to arouse the attention of several men. In the hotel bathroom, as those several men are stripping off, Tony, the director of the porno-shoot, wearing a brown tracksuit top, explains the rules: 'No touching below the waist,' he says, 'and if you're going to come, just put your hand up, so I can get the shot.' He understands that the statement he has just made contains a humorous play on words, so he gives a smile. Some of the men wear the white, expressionless masks we've offered them to protect their identities, and look like the chorus in a naturist performance of a Greek play. Then in various states of excitement they wander into the bedroom. Some men are flabby and pale, others are bronzed and toned, one has a gold stud in his belly button. They crowd around the bed and Faye goes to work on them, sometimes with her mouth, sometimes with her hand, and sometimes with both hands, like a crazed milk-maid late for market. Tony films them, and we film Tony, and we film Faye and the men being filmed by Tony. In an interview beforehand, Faye had laughed like a horse as she told us stories of going home on the bus with sperm in her hair, or finding some in her ear a few days later. She'd said, 'Sometimes when I get up off that bed I look like a melted candle.' I use that image in her song, which she's happy to sing for us while she goes about her business, croaking out one verse at a time as she surfaces for air. Some of what we film will obviously be too much for network television – even for Channel 4 – so instead of following the scene to its very climax we eventually cut away to a packet of Tesco's wet wipes on the windowsill.

The men who take part in the Bukkake sessions are volunteers, recruited through magazines and websites. Some are unemployed perverts with nothing better to do, others are businessmen attending in their lunch hour. They do not pay to take part, neither are they paid. The pornography people get what they want – a Bukkake film – and the participants are rewarded with the opportunity of masturbating on to a well-known porn star, which is considered by most of them to be more than adequate remuneration. They also get to appear in a pornographic film. So just as Faye can argue that she is an actress, so these men could argue, possibly, if push came to shove, that they are in fact film stars, and not simply wankers.

Song of the Songbird

♫

Sleep, little chick, through stormy weather,
mammy flew off and lost a feather,
but ever she's coming with corn in her beak,
so sleep, little songbird, sleep.

Sleep, little chick, through midnight dark,
the trap was set and mammy got caught
but never no trap will ever her keep
so sleep, little songbird, sleep.

Soon I'll be climbing into the sky,
sleep, little songbird, close your eyes,
yon hunting hawks won't never get me
sleep, little songbird, don't forget me . . .

Sleep, little songbird, mammy did wrong,
but ever she's calling, singing her song,
and ever you're cradled in mammy's nest,
under mammy's wing, under mammy's breast.

♫

Sung by Maggie in the film *Songbirds*. (Century Films/ Channel 4, 2005).

On the Road 2

The owner of The Great Outdoors is getting flustered. He's kitted out Everest expeditions. He's equipped polar explorers with sleeping bags. He's supplied trekkers with everything they need to cross the Sahara. He may even have sold sealskin jackets to the Inuit and loincloths to Amazonian Indians for all I know, but he's never sold a pair of boots to a writer.

'Where are you going?' he wants to know.

'Surtsey.'

'OK. I see. Fine.'

He hasn't heard of it. I watch for the light going on in the back of his head but it remains dark. He isn't one of us. However, a man in his position can't be seen to have gaps in his geographical knowledge, and the last thing he wants is to lose face in front of his other customers: rugged, *Touching the Void* types trying on skintight thermal vests in front of the full-length mirror.

'And what's the purpose of the trip?'

'Poetry,' I say, unhelpfully.

Now we really are in uncharted territory. He looks again at the selection of footwear in my size, big clodhopping leather things with fittings for crampons and snowshoes. Then from the bottom shelf he produces something in brown suede, more like a trainer than a boot.

'Well, these are pretty lightweight,' he says.

I'm remembering all this as I stand in the lobby of the Reykjavik Hotel, waiting for a taxi to take me to the coastguard station, about a mile from the city centre. The boots are very comfortable; so is the fleece, though I still haven't worked out why the pockets of serious out-door jackets must zip from top to bottom (to stop your car keys falling out when you're dangling upside down from Mont Blanc?), and I'm not sure about the black nylon leggings. I get chatting with a couple of Brits, two ski-tanned guys from Kent who've come north to drive a Land Rover across a glacier and canoe down a waterfall.

'What about you? Where are you heading?'

'Surtsey.'

I wait for a response but there isn't any. The world is clearly divided into two groups: those who've heard of the place and those who haven't. One group that spent its childhood watching *Blue Peter*, *John Craven's Newsround*, public information films and educational documentaries about volcanic eruptions in the North Atlantic, and another group who watched ITV.

On 14 November 1963, fishermen on a trawler off the Westman Islands, about twenty miles from the south coast of Iceland, noticed bubbles in the sea and jets of steam rising from the water. They thought they might be looking at a submarine in trouble; in fact they were witnessing the birth of a new land. Over the coming months and years an underwater volcano continued to erupt, the millions of tons of molten magma and ash eventually forming the second biggest island in the archipelago and rather conveniently extending Iceland's fishing territory by a good few miles. Realizing the scientific importance of their newly acquired territory, Icelandic geologists, vulcanologists and seismologists were crawling all over it before the crust had set, and at a meeting of whoever decides these kind of things, the island was eventually named after the Norse god of fire, Surtur. Other events of that year included the assassination of John F. Kennedy and mass vaccination against measles. Less newsworthy was the arrival in this world of the poet Simon Armitage. Like a discrete number of others, I've always been conscious that I share a birth year with a lump of rock, and seem to belong to a generation for whom Surtsey is a kind of psychological touchstone. If newsreel and archive film footage made me aware of its infancy and its adolescence, being a geography graduate also meant I received regular updates on Surtsey's development throughout my late teens and early twenties. And in my more recent role as a poet, as reports have come in of Surtsey's midlife crisis and literal struggle to keep its head above water, the island has taken on an even bigger significance: it has become a metaphor. As someone who was once told that the bones in his pelvis and spine weren't going to last the distance, I've been interested to learn that my geological twin brother is also crumbling away. And for the first time in forty years, we're going to meet.

The crew of the coastguard's shiny red helicopter don't ask why I'm going to Surtsey. They're all wearing heavy-duty ear-protectors to blank out the scream of the engine and they're completely engrossed in their gadgets. The pilot taps one of the several dozen dials with a gloved finger.

The co-pilot flicks a switch and turns a knob. The winch-man adjusts levers and handles somewhere behind me, and sitting next to me, the navigator boots up his laptop. A map of Iceland appears on his screen. Then, as we leave the coast, a map of nothing, which I guess is the sea. I've been in that sea once before, on a trawler, and puked up for nine hours. This time I'm glad to be experiencing it from above.

Cartographically speaking, Surtsey looks remarkably like a human head. The main points of eruption left two deep, empty craters, which from the air look like sunken eye sockets. Above them, the mass of lava formed two sizable hills – two raised eyebrows, joined by a narrow ridge, like the bridge of a nose or the brow. To the bottom end of the island a spit or ness has developed, like a long thin chin sporting a goatee beard. Imagine the skull-like face in Munch's *Scream*, two and a half miles long and a mile wide, and you're getting the picture. We land somewhere around the left cheek, on a small concrete helicopter pad in a field of soft black cinders, then duck under the rotor blades and scramble towards the hut, one of two buildings on the island. As huts go, this is towards the top of the range, but nothing that you couldn't find in a decent garden centre or DIY superstore. The door isn't locked of course. There's stuff here worth nicking but no one to nick it. In fact, judging by the amount of black, sooty dust inside I have to wonder if the door was not only unlocked but left wide open for the winter.

In an ideal world I might have come here alone, and done the Robinson Crusoe thing, and made a big song and dance about solitude. But this isn't an exercise in voluntary isolation, and in any case, the powers that be weren't going to let a poet stumble around their precious island without a couple of experts to tell him which flowers he shouldn't stand on and how to dispose of his Kit-Kat wrappers. It's for that reason I'm flanked by Dr Ármann Höskuldsson and Dr Olgeir Sigmarsson, both experts on volcanoes. As well as my two guides, I'm accompanied by crack Radio 4 features producer and hard-core birdwatcher Tim Dee. He carries a furry microphone in one hand to record whatever I come out with, and a pair of serious-looking binoculars in the other. Power supply being spectacularly non-existent on Surtsey, he's also weighed down with several magazine clips of AA batteries which he is conscence-bound to return to the UK for recycling. Throughout the trip he trudges alongside me while I float from rock to rock in my breathable jacket and fairy-boots, thinking my poetic thoughts.

From a cupboard Ármann produces a couple of brooms and while he runs the Icelandic flag up the pole outside we begin sweeping. When I ask where the toilet is he points to a long-handled spade propped in the corner. If I'd wanted a proper, old-fashioned adventure, I guess this is the moment when it starts to come true. Four of us in a toiletless hut on an uninhabited island in the middle of the sea. Also, as I'm putting the brushes back, I notice a pile of items not usually found in a domestic broom cupboard, such as flares, ropes, blankets, a heavy-duty medicine chest and other survivalist paraphernalia. The sense of adventure is broken, however, when my mobile phone goes off and a teacher in Leicestershire wants to know if I'd consider writing a poem for the opening of their new arts block on National Poetry Day. Back in Huddersfield I can't get a signal without leaning out of the attic window with a metal coat hanger, but here in the middle of nowhere, for reasons I can't fathom, Vodafone are open for business.

After eating, we make a three-hour circuit of the island, taking in both of its peaks, the cliffs to the north, the lava field to the south and the western crater. It culminates in a stroll through an area of lush grass and top-heavy, cow-eyed daisies. I casually christen it 'the Meadow', and later in the day I'm chuffed to hear Ármann inadvertently refer to it by the same name. We talk about which types of grasses and flowers have managed to get a toehold on Surtsey. He tells me that when the first plant sprouted through the inhospitable grit it had to be sent off to Sweden to be 'determined'. The Swedes are very good at that kind of thing, apparently. To the amazement of the boffins, it turned out to be nothing less than a tomato plant – not exactly indigenous to this part of the world. After a lot of head-scratching the embarrassing truth had to be acknowledged. In all likelihood the tomato seed hadn't been blown here from Africa or transported in the primary feathers of a herring gull, but deposited on Surtsey's virgin soil by a well-fed scientist evacuating his bowels. Thereafter new orders were posted, instructing all visitors to bury their deposits well below the surface. Hence the shovel and its notably long handle.

Whether true or false, the anecdote leads us, one way or another, to a lengthier, more general discussion on the subject of human detritus. The earth is in a bad way. For our parents, environmentalism was a new, almost exotic concept, like the arrival of prawns in the local super-market. But we've got no excuse. And Surtsey, as Ármann points out over the last of the vodka that evening, is a microcosm of earth. Against all the odds, bacteria, insects, flowers and birds have flourished here. Out of nothing, life has evolved. Later, when Tim isn't fancying a kittiwake or tracking the flight of a fulmar, I point the binoculars at some red and green blobs down on the spit, thinking they're a colourful species of jellyfish laid up till high tide. But stumbling towards them, I discover they're not part of the local zoology at all but net floats, hundreds of them, like giant bowling balls, washed up with tons of other unbiodegradable maritime junk, including ropes, crates, polystyrene fish boxes, tyres and various unidentifiable rusty bits of ship heaved on to the rocks. More pointedly, as we walk back towards the cliffs we find a bird on a rock, a beautifully sleek guillemot that stands its ground as we get within five or six feet. It doesn't fly because its feathers are gummed together with crude oil. There's nothing we can do but turn our backs and walk away. To try and forget it, Ármann points south and tells me that between here and Antarctica there's nothing but the sea. Nothing but water and whatever crap we've thrown into it, that is, and judging by the amount that has found its way to this protected sanctuary in the middle of nowhere, there's a lot of it out there.

Later still, with the smell of pasta and meat stirring something inside me, I utter the words I'd been hoping not to say. 'I think I need to use the shovel,' I announce, and set off into the lava field looking for a suitable location.

Bearing in mind the parable of the tomato seed, and remembering an apple core I munched a couple of days ago, I dig deep. If Surtsey really is a kind of scientific Garden of Eden, I don't want to be the serpent responsible for the introduction of a Granny Smith.

We make a final tour, me and Tim in the footsteps of Ármann and Olgeir, who drop samples of volcanic rock into a plastic bag and make notes in their pocketbooks. One sample is discarded, though – a fragment of concrete from the former lighthouse on the island's highest peak. They've built several, but the 200 mph winds that regularly race across Surtsey create an instant vacuum within any structure, and the buildings have a nasty habit of imploding. It would be nice to think that the decimated hut says something about man's futile attempt to conquer the forces of nature. But the hill has been recolonized with a new hut, bigger and stronger, and in any case, since the advent of GPS navigation, ships can manoeuvre around these treacherous islands without the aid of illumination. The small piece of man-made stone has no geological importance, but to me it has plenty of symbolic relevance, and after Olgeir has tossed it over his shoulder I pocket it. Then it's time to leave. I've packed my kitbag and written a poem in the visitors' book. I can hear the helicopter buzzing in a distant cloud.

Now that the scientists have learned what they need to know about Surtsey, there's talk of opening it up as a tourist attraction. Boat trips, perhaps, guided walks even, and for those willing to fork out for the full package, a candlelit stew and a sleepless night in the one-star hut.

Personally I won't be coming back, because I've learned my lesson. I'd arrived here with the vain idea of comparing my own lifespan to that of this small land mass, but as one of my poetic forebears had already pointed out, no man is an island. Also, I'd overestimated the rate of Surtsey's disintegration by a factor of many. The place might well be falling apart, but when I ask Ármann who will survive the longest – me or it – his deadpan answer kills the comparison once and for all:

'The favourite is Surtsey, unless you're planning to live for another ten thousand years.'

On the other hand, what the rest of the blue planet will look like in that time can only be guessed at. And if hiking around this lump of new land can give us any sense of what we're doing to the old one, then I'm all for opening up the border. A word of warning, though. If you find yourself strolling through an area described on the map as the Meadow, a sort of earthly paradise thick with wild flowers and a single fruit tree growing in the centre, don't eat the apple.

*

It's 1996, and I'm with Glyn Maxwell at the Poetry Society in London, launching a book we've written about Iceland. It's a humid, un-Icelandic summer evening and too many of us are packed into the small basement of 22 Betterton Street, friends and family mainly. After a lot of drinks, someone tells us we should read from the book. Looking down at the poem on the page, I suddenly notice it contains an expletive.

'There's a word in this poem I've never said in front of my mother before,' I say.

From within a cloud of pipe smoke, out of the side of his mouth but loud enough to be heard, my dad says, 'Is it thank you?'

The Fall
Huddersfield University
2 October 2005

```
HUDDERSFIELD UNIVERSITY S.U.
QUEENSGATE, HUDDERSFIELD, HD1 3DH
SUN  2nd   OCT 05    7:30 PM

WISE MOVES PRESENTS
THE FALL
+ SPECIAL GUEST JOHN COOPER CLARKE

TICKETS £15.00 plus booking fee
```

I learned to write poetry at Huddersfield Poly. Not as a student – they were more like evening classes, run by Peter Sansom. They took place in a tatty old lecture room or in the staff bar, with the clack of snooker balls in the background and an underemployed barman swilling out the drip trays. And I saw all my first bands at Huddersfield Poly, sometimes in the Great Hall but mostly in the student union, a sort of purpose built fire hazard, like an enlarged shoebox with a ceiling so low that an energetic, pogoing punk could leave the impression of his head in the highly combustible polystyrene tiles. At the Vapors gig, I watched in fascinated horror as the big skinheads at the front delivered round after round of sooty, eggy West Yorkshire phlegm in the direction of the band, who carried on, not exactly regardless, but in the face of torrential circumstances. I don't imagine the Vapors have fond memories of Huddersfield, or any of the towns either side of the M62 in the so-called Northern Punk Belt where gobbing was common practice. When they played 'Turning Japanese' the spitting, supposedly a kind of homage, reached its climax, and I can still picture frontman Dave Fenton (a former solicitor) trying to form a chord with his right hand as the strings of his guitar dripped with snot. As tributes go, I hope this kind of adulation never becomes popular on the poetry circuit.

The Poly is now Huddersfield University. It occupies the same site but many of the old brick-and-concrete buildings have made way for structures of glass and steel. It might be twenty years since I was last in the student union, and it takes me a while to find, not because it has moved but because it has changed. In fact once I'm in it, I still don't know I'm there. What was once a kind of dilapidated common room now appears to be a video arcade, like the Game Zone in a motorway service station, and what was once a bar is now a shop. A supermarket, in fact. Young people queue in front of me with cleaning products and bottles of half-decent wine in their baskets. There's no law to say that a students' union must be a place of stale sweat and radical thought, and no reason why university service-users should go uncatered for, but it seems odd to me that the hub of activity in a seat of learning should be a Somerfield or a Spar.

'Is this the right place to buy tickets to see The Fall?' I ask the woman on the till. She doesn't know. She's new, and she'll have to check with Mary, or Betty, or someone else in a stripy apron. Mary or Betty aren't sure either.

'What is it for, love?'

'The Fall.'

'What is that?'

'A band.'

'Like a group?'

'Yes.'

'Playing a concert?'

'Yes.'

'I think you buy them online.'

'I phoned up and they said I could buy them here.'

'Oh. Funny.'

Betty or Mary will now have to ask Sheila or Margaret. There are seven or eight patient but unimpressed students behind, waiting to pay for hairspray or *Top Gear* magazine. I feel old and disreputable. I feel dodgy, as if I've asked for something from under the counter. And under the counter is where the tickets turn out to be, in a little lockable tin, with the scratch cards and the books of stamps.

'Now, love, how many?'

'One.'

On top of the wad of tickets there's a piece of card, on which a running total of sales has been kept. Even from three feet away, I can see that the tally is sixteen. The scorecard is made up of two columns.

'Are you staff or student?' she asks me.

'Neither.'

'What are you then?'

'Er . . . I'm just . . . you know.'

'Oh. Funny.'

She writes the word 'Other' on the card, and with a slash of her blue biro registers my single purchase in her new category. Then I'm out of the shop and away.

As it turns out I didn't need a ticket at all because good-hearted John Cooper Clarke has put me on the guest list. I have a drink with him backstage, backstage being the upstairs corridor of a suite of offices, but clear off before Mark E. Smith arrives. Famously intolerant of liggers and even less charitable towards his admirers, I don't want to fall under the mean eye of his disapproval or be pinioned on the end of his flick-knife tongue. I did speak to him once, in 1995, at the Crossing Border spoken word festival in The Hague. We were on the same bill. I was reading poems, and he, by his own admission and in his own words, didn't know what the fuck he was doing.

'I really like your stuff,' I said. I might even have appended the word 'man' to the end of that sentence.

'Got a light, cock?'

'No, sorry.'

'I don't know what the fuck I'm doing here. What are you doing?'

'Reading poems.'

'I think they think I'm some kind of fuckin' . . .' To a Dutch stagehand: 'Ey, got a light, cock?'

(In Dutch) 'Pardon?'

'Never mind. I don't know what the fuck I'm gonna do.'

'You're on in half an hour, aren't you?'

'What did Bargeld do?'

'Something with a little tape recorder.'

'Did he? Bastard. That's what I'm gonna do. They think I'm some kind of fuckin' . . . Blixa? Ey, Blixa, lend us that fucking tape machine.'

The Crossing Border website talks about 'often extra-ordinary happenings, artists committing themselves to the audience, without the support of their band and armed solely with their texts'. Half an hour after our 'conver-sation', Smith shuffled on to the stage, stationed himself at a little card table, played unidentifiable music from Blixa Bargeld's hand-held cassette player into the micro-phone and read headlines from the *Daily Mirror*. He was laughing as he did it and I watched him from the wings. Henry Rollins was strutting around at the same event, showing off his thick neck and tattoos. So was David Thomas from Pere Ubu, who dismissed his fellow musicians mid-set and performed a breathtaking solo version of Iggy Pop's 'The Passenger' on a squeeze box, wearing a cooking apron.

My problem with The Fall is that I really *do* like their stuff. I mean, I really *really* like it. I own a great fat slab of it, and it isn't like owning a stamp collection or a leather-bound boxed set of first edition Dickens. I use it. It's functional. Practical. It's utilitarian. I play it whenever possible, and it sounds better and better all the time. I don't own it all. Counting re-releases and imports, there are more Fall albums than ex-Fall members, which is saying something. But I've got everything that matters, and to me it matters a great deal. On Radio 3's *Private Passions* in 2002 I made some polite and informed choices. Essentially a classical music programme, as well as Ravel and Hugo Wolf I chose Scott Walker and Radiohead. Between John Tavener's 'The Lamb' and Duruflé's *Requiem*, I even managed to slip in Serious Drinking's 'Spirit of 66'. 'Perhaps you'd better explain it,' said presenter Michael Berkeley. The studio was in the attic of his house somewhere in London, and the records were layed in through a modern speaker encased in an old-fashioned gramophone. The song, from the album *The Revolution Starts at Closing Time*, is basically a punk anthem listing England's World Cup-winning heroes, barked out, terrace-style, by Norwich's finest. Asked why I'd chosen

that record, I told him that if the poetry ever went down the toilet, it reminded me that I could always resume my career as an intercontinental football hooligan. I've never actually been to a game of football outside these shores. He laughed, but rather nervously, I thought. The track I really wanted to play, though, was vetoed over the kitchen table earlier that morning without a note of it being struck. Deemed too long, it was The Fall's 'Frightened', from the album *Live at the Witch Trials*, though a few years later I did get a chance to share this track with BBC listeners on Radio 4's *Armitage and Moore's Guide to Song*. A cult programme (i.e. short-lived), it consisted mainly of me banging on about lyrics and Allan Moore, a lecturer in musicology at Sussex University, banging on about music and occasionally banging on the piano to illustrate his point. I explained how 'Frightened' was a master-piece, full of metaphysical detail and breathless, climbing chord progressions which perfectly represented those fearful states of mind so closely associated with post-amphetamine paranoia. Allan nodded in agreement.

'So do you like it?' I asked him.

'Can't bear it,' he said.

Some say that *Fall Heads Roll*, a recent Fall album, is their best ever. After three decades of listening to them I've stopped trying to compare. The Fall came together when I was fourteen and they're still together today, so my interest in music is entirely spanned by their output. I can't empathize with anyone who doesn't admire or appreciate The Fall. If you don't like them, you're wrong. But I'm not sure I like Mark E. Smith. I guess that's OK. He doesn't really exist to be liked. Otherwise, why would he have peed in a bucket at the ICA? And why would he have gurned like a gumby on *Newsnight* when an ill-warned and unprepared Gavin Esler tried to interview him about the death of John Peel? Also, to admire The Fall is to arouse his suspicions. Praise is to Smith what garlic is to a vampire. Cynicism seems his only ideology – he is against EVERYTHING. And, at times, EVERY-ONE. He doesn't just manage The Fall, he is The Fall. He's often described as totalitarian or a dictator, but to me those terms are too exotic. They smack of enigmatic leaders in turbulent countries with complex relationships to the rest of the world. To my mind, Smith is more like the owner of a family-run furniture manufacturer's in provincial northern England, bullying his staff and mocking his customers. Employees come and go. Some stay loyal for decades, others flounce out after a few hours. Some leave with a mumbled word of gratitude, some with a flea in their ear, and some with a cuff round the head or a boot up the arse. The boss is intimidating, maniacal and infuriatingly unpredictable, but on one subject he remains utterly consistent, and that subject is work. Hard work. The Fall are a working band. You do your shift. Put the time in. If they're not touring, they're recording. If they're not recording, they're touring. Two albums a year isn't unheard of. The Fall make bands like U2, who've been around for about the same time, look like a bunch of lilo-loafing, lotus-eating slackers by comparison.

At Huddersfield University, there has obviously been an upward trend in ticket sales since the seventeen recorded on Betty or Mary's cardboard spreadsheet. Some are Student. Some are Staff. But most are Others, I'm pleased to say, including a gang of lads from the village I didn't even know were into any kind of music, let alone The Fall. My old English teacher is here, and so is his teenage son. And two or three faces I recognize from a Skids gig, a mere twenty-eight years ago. John Cooper Clarke is John Cooper Clarke. I mean, he really is John Cooper Clarke – same haircut, same glasses, same poems, same brilliance. He once told me he'd turned down a part in the film *24 Hour Party People*, a decision he now very much regretted.

'What was the part?'

'Me.'

And The Fall are The Fall. I mean, they're not The Fall – different drummer, different guitarists, different girlfriend on keyboards – but Smith is there, and as he once said, 'If it's just me and your granny on bongos, it's a Fall gig.' He chews something throughout the show – his tongue? Not Nicorette, surely. And he wanders around the stage with his hands in his pockets, snarling and muttering, slurring and cursing, grumbling and grinding his teeth, while the band plug away, workmanlike, through 'Pacifying Drug' and 'What About Us?'. When the throbbing bassline of 'Blindness' finds a resonant frequency somewhere in the solar plexus, it's less like listening to music and more like receiving an internal massage. At one stage, Smith walks into the wings and makes a life-mask of his face by covering his head with the curtain, and sings into the microphone through the heavy cloth. Apart from that, it's just the standard oddness.

★

To mark thirty years in the business The Fall play a birthday gig in Manchester, with rumours in the press and on the internet of a private party afterwards. It's a gig that any self-respecting Fall fan should be seen at, and wangling an invite into the after-show shindig should be the immediate priority of anyone who considers themselves an aficionado. But today my obligations lie elsewhere. So instead of seeing The Fall playing a landmark event on home soil and maybe getting to trade a few comments with the man himself, I'm going birdwatching in Norfolk.

I'm not a proper birdwatcher. Tim Dee is a proper birdwatcher. And Mark Cocker is a proper birdwatcher; he could birdwatch for England, which is pretty much what he was doing when he put together the great tome of work that is *Birds Britannica*. In the flooded meadow behind Mark's house we watch Chinese water deer and barn owls in the evening light before turning in for an early night, because we need to be up and off by 4 a.m. The object of the exercise is to spot as many species of birds in a single day as possible. If other teams of birdwatchers were taking part this activity would be known as a bird race, and would be highly competitive. But today it's just us three against nature, with Mark at the wheel, Tim with the map and me in the back seat with the Mars bars and the naïve comments. We begin in a wood, looking for golden pheasant, and Tim has already recorded about twenty ticks on the sheet before I've spotted a single living creature. This is because a great deal of birdwatching is done not with the eyes but with the ears, and it's perfectly legitimate to say that a particular bird has been 'seen' when really it has only been heard. Near an overgrown gateway, Mark describes to me in whispers the subtle difference between the song of the blackcap and that of the garden warbler. When you've been doing this as long as he has, it's as obvious as distinguishing Motorhead from the Proclaimers, apparently. But to my ear, and to my frustration, the songs are almost inseparable. Mark tells me we're not far from the location where the two Soham girls were buried, and in this shadowy place at this haunting hour of the morning, it's easy to imagine looking up and seeing through the timber the silhouette of a man hurrying back to his car with a spade in his hands.

The day is long and varied. Some sites reveal nothing, such as Lynford Stag Park in Breckland which provides not a single firecrest. Others deliver their promise: hawfinches at Lynford Arboretum, and bug-eyed, prehistoric-looking stone curlews finding a safe haven between the bomb craters and tank-tracks on MoD land at Foxhole Heath. Yet more locations throw up the unexpected, like the pair of kingfishers that flash beneath the stone bridge at Santon Downham. But are we three men engaged in a noble and improving pursuit, or are we the Goodies, stumbling and bumbling around low-lying England with binoculars and a Thermos? At one point, I'm either so fuddled by tiredness or so excited by spotting something better than a starling, I blurt out, 'Eagle!' In fact it's a barn owl. Barn owls are good, not to be sniffed at, but they're not eagles. East Anglian eagles are very rare. All day long my phone vibrates with barbed and sarky text messages from mates at home, because rather than watching England's opener in the World Cup in Germany, I'm twitching. (As things turn out, my day is more enjoyable than witnessing the scrambled 1–0 victory over Paraguay.) It culminates on a dung heap on Beacon Hill near North Creake, watching a male and female Montagu's harrier soaring and wheeling through the twilight several fields away, until the light fades. Back at Mark's house, total exhaustion has muddied my conversation and confused my thoughts. Ideas fly into each other and crash. Notions migrate and don't come back. The Fall might be doing an encore round about now. Just as I'm hitting the pillow and falling into a deep, comatose sleep, I run through the complete list of birds seen by Armitage, Cocker and Dee on 10 June 2006:

Scenario (4:57)
Assume (3:16)
Pacifying Joint (4:09)
Theme from Sparta FC (4:36)
Mountain Energei (6:22)
Reformation (3:56)
What About Us? (8:14)
I Can Hear the Grass Grow (3:02)
Wrong Place, Right Time (4:21)
Bo Demmick (4:15)
White Line Fever (3:05)
Mr Pharmacist (2:28)
Blindness (11:07)
Encore Call (2:54)
Midnight in Aspen (4:15)
Systematic Abuse (8:35)

And here's the set list from The Fall's birthday bash at New Century Hall, Corporation Street, Manchester. It was, as one of their many websites points out, an essential gig for any self-respecting fan, but one that I can now only dream of:

1. Whitethroat
2. Blackbird
3. House sparrow
4. Great tit
5. Wood pigeon
6. Wren
7. Jackdaw
8. Grey heron
9. Rook
10. Carrion crow
11. Mallard
12. Pheasant
13. Starling
14. Blackcap
15. Goldcrest
16. Chaffinch
17. Song thrush
18. Great spotted woodpecker
19. Chiffchaff
20. Treecreeper
21. Garden warbler
22. Skylark
23. Blue tit
24. Mistle thrush
25. Stock dove

26. Pied wagtail
27. Willow warbler
28. Cuckoo
29. Linnet
30. Yellowhammer
31. Curlew
32. Tree pipit
33. Lesser black-backed gull
34. Shelduck
35. Redstart
36. Coot
37. Lapwing
38. Mute swan
39. Little grebe
40. Gadwall
41. Greylag goose
42. Egyptian goose
43. Moorhen
44. Jay
45. Coal tit
46. Woodlark
47. Green woodpecker
48. Goldfinch
49. Magpie
50. Greenfinch
51. Grey wagtail
52. Long-tailed tit
53. Kingfisher
54. Swallow
55. Robin
56. Siskin

57. Collared dove
58. House martin
59. Eagle (OK, Barn owl)
60. Dunnock
61. Kestrel
62. Hawfinch
63. Stone curlew
64. Cormorant
65. Reed warbler
66. Reed bunting
67. Common tern
68. Shoveler
69. Sedge warbler
70. Marsh harrier
71. Hobby
72. Golden oriole
73. Turtle dove
74. Canada goose
75. Buzzard
76. Black-headed gull
77. Bearded tit
78. Little egret
79. Ruddy duck
80. Wigeon
81. Little ringed plover
82. Oystercatcher
83. Redshank
84. Herring gull
85. Meadow pipit
86. Common gull
87. Little gull

88. Great black-backed gull
89. Teal
90. Pochard
91. Avocet
92. Knot
93. Black-tailed godwit
94. Bar-tailed godwit
95. Ringed plover
96. Mediterranean gull
97. Turnstone
98. Sand martin
99. Little tern
100. Sandwich tern
101. Common scoter
102. Kittiwake
103. Gannet
104. Dunlin
105. Sanderling
106. Manx shearwater
107. Grey partridge
108. Corn bunting
109. Montagu's harrier
110. Lesser whitethroat

On the Road 3

Someone phones up from a programme called *Regency House Party*. It's a bit like *Big Brother*, but set in a stately home in Herefordshire with participants living in strict early-nineteenth-century conditions. They want a 'Lord Byron-type person' to come along one night and read a few poems: am I interested? I explain that my basic starting position with any gig is that I don't do tricks. So I won't, for instance, get dressed up as a Romantic poet with a club foot and act out a simulated sex scene with my half-sister, but I'm happy to turn up as myself. Eventually they phone back and it's a deal.

The location is Kentchurch Court, a large country pile and sprawling estate at the end of a long track near the Welsh border. It must be one of the most beautiful and unspoilt parts of Britain, which is another way of saying I get lost several times trying to find it. On the outside of a temporary perimeter fence, TV people are milling about with clipboards, walkie-talkies and disposable cups. Stepping through the gate should be like stepping back in time, but the illusion is compromised by the constant presence of a cameraman and his sidekicks, plus the fact that two of the catering team are having a major bust-up in the downstairs kitchen using a vocabulary not appropriate to the period. Once the camera is rolling, I am 'received' by a Mr Darcy lookalike, who, judging by his impressive sideburns and Merchant Ivory body language, has clearly taken the project to heart. In his appointed role as lord of the manor he guides me towards a drawing room where I am introduced to the other house guests. Then we go through for dinner. In keeping with the spirit and rules of the occasion, dinner is peacock, and like most of the peacocks in this world, below the display of colourful feathers there isn't much of it. And it tastes like chicken, of course.

In common with other programmes of its type, the object of *Regency House Party* is romance. This isn't a stated ambition, but looking around the dining room and making table talk, it's clear that nearly everyone here is youngish, unattached and on the right side of ugly. In other words, up for it. More than anything, this is a dating game. However, due to the restrictions placed on the women-folk, it's difficult to see how even the most innocuous form of courtship could take place. The fairer sex are confined indoors for much of the day, and on the rare moments when they are allowed to mingle with the males of the species they are accompanied by fierce-looking chaperones. Behind closed doors they practise the gentle arts of embroidery and hair-brushing, while through the windows they watch the young men wandering about in the woods, loafing in the sun, slurping port on the terrace, lopping watermelons in half with ceremonial swords and generally enjoying the freedom of the grounds. Any feelings of a tender nature between the men and the women must be communicated by written message to be scrutinized and edited by the frosty matrons.

As if social segregation weren't enough, the women

are also physically confined, being trussed in corsets and girdles which must make breathing difficult and eating virtually impossible. So despite the prodigious amount of uplifted bosom and enforced cleavage on display, the possibility of a twenty-first-century relationship blossoming under Regency conditions seems limited indeed. There is meat in the butcher's window, but the shop is closed. Worse still, those women allocated the roles of poor relation and unendowed niece seem destined never to see the light of day let alone make contact with anyone. Their Regency House experience must be less like playing the part of the heroine in a romantic novel and more like an audition for the part of Mrs Rochester. Amongst the women, already cooped up here for several weeks before my arrival, feelings are running high, especially after supper when they are packed off to bed while the gentlemen kick back with brandy and cigars.

But the character enjoying the most liberty, it seems to me, is the Regency House hermit, left to his own devices for twenty-four hours a day and living in a shack somewhere on the grounds. He's a lanky, hairy guy of uncertain age and uncertain veracity. Is he really communing with woodland creatures and watching the sunrise every morning, or is he blowing dope and sleeping with the production assistant? A hermit in real life as well as on telly, he tells me he has forsaken all worldly goods and for many months of the year has no fixed address, preferring to live in peoples' gardens. In return for such lodging he dispenses wit and wisdom to anyone who enquires, and during dinner parties is occasionally invited to the table as an object of curiosity and a topic of conversation.

His appetite for suffering might be stronger than I give him credit for, but I make the assumption that a country gazebo or a suburban potting shed at the very least would be the preferred accommodation for his hermiting, and that he might not be as keen to bed down in the wheely-bin store at the back of a Halifax council estate. (Upon further research into modern-day hermits, I'm surprised to find how many of them have websites. I'm interested in this way of life because of my surname. Armitage is derived from hermitage. It could be that some of my distant ancestors spent their life lurking in the undergrowth, sleeping under the stars and eating hedgehogs.)

In a vault beneath the house the production team have recreated a version of the Hellfire Club. Among burning torches and flowing wine I read a few poems, none of them remotely appropriate to the evening, it occurs to me as I wade through them. Then belly dancers appear, scantily clad, shaking their stuff. The eyeballs of the sex-starved gentlemen, now popping from their skulls, show almost as much of their circumference as the eyeballs of several sheep being served on a platter as part of our Turkish supper. Feeling a little queasy and more and more surplus to requirements, I step outside for a breath of fresh air. Like Mr Benn after one of his little adventures, I'm suddenly back in the real world, and no one seems bothered if I remain in the present day, so I sneak off into the night. In the end, the decision to wear a Ben Sherman shirt and black jeans rather than pantaloons and a frilly blouse pays dividends: I get a fee, half a day's birdwatching in thickest Herefordshire, and (as far as I know) I don't appear in the programme. Result.

Down on Mary Street

♫

Here come the mufti squad to scissor off my clothes.
Here come the goon squad with the stun-gun and the hose.
They'll put me in an arm-lock and they'll trigger back my thumb.
They'd pull my fingernails out but they're bitten to the stump.

Who me – I thought temazepams were little jelly sweets.
Who me – I thought diazepams were after-dinner treats.

Here comes scary Mary – someone hit the fire alarm.
She's cut her throat and gone and slashed a bar code in her arm.
She went up in a ball of flames inside the padded cell –
but we were drinking tea and couldn't hear the panic bell.

Who me – I thought a prison was a fancy second home.
Who me – I thought a banquet was a bucket full of bones.

And I'm oh so sorry that I spat my blood at you,
and I'm oh so oh so sorry that I split your head in two,
see I was fifteen when it happened and I didn't even bleed,
and I'm still down there,
      I'm still down there,
        I'm down on Mary Street.

Here comes some punter in his swanky new car.
Here comes the lube-tube and the weightlifting bar.
A thing like that could leave a woman tattered and torn.
You're screwing with my baby and it isn't even born.

Who me – I thought a national park was a prison yard.
Who me – I thought a flick knife was a cashpoint card.

Don't give her back her life she won't know what to do.
Don't send her back outside she wouldn't have a clue.
Don't leave the door ajar she's better off inside.
Don't say I said so BUT THEY'RE ABSOLUTELY RIGHT.

And I'm oh so sorry that I trashed this place,
and I'm oh so oh so sorry that I'm always in your face,
see I was fifteen when it started and I didn't even bleed,
and I'm still down there,
      I'm still down there,
          I'm down on Mary Street.

♫

Sung by 'Scary' Mary in the film *Songbirds* (Century Films/
Channel 4, 2005).

Crispy Ambulance
Live on a Hot August Night
FACBN4

We're making a film. It's about me. Following the *Picture of Britain* series presented by David Dimbleby, each region has been asked to profile one of its artists. I am THE NORTH. We have high hopes for the film – a thirty-minute piece to be shown on BBC1 after the *Ten O'Clock News* – but a small budget. So instead of a cameraman, a sound recordist, a researcher and a director, we have Keith. Keith is a lovely bloke who used to be the drummer with the Utah Saints. He has lots of energy but not much time, and lots of ideas, most of which are scribbled on the back of a serviette after one of our planning meetings. He also has a lovely assistant with him, a media studies student at Leeds University. She's on a steep learning curve. My dad, whose house has become our canteen for the week, is not impressed with the set-up.

'Who's that lass?'

'Production assistant.'

'What kind of production assistant dun't have a pen or a watch?'

'She's on a bit of a learning curve.'

'She's on the bloody wall of death more like.'

At an early point in the project, thinking about a particular obsession of mine, we decide that a tyre should be a recurring motif in the film, rolling freely through the moors and roads of the Colne Valley, as it does in one of the poems, thus leading us from one scene to the next. We're blessed with good weather, so late one morning we decide to film on top of Pule Hill, the enigmatic and iconic hill above Marsden where Mount Road meets the A62. From the top you can see the Humber Bridge to the east and the Blackpool Tower to the west. You'd need a telescope and a spectacularly clear day but, on paper at least, that's the view. Pule Hill is 1,434 feet above sea level, a fact registered by your heart rate and your sweat glands if you've walked to the summit carrying a tyre in your arms. Camera batteries are also heavy, but they've been left in the car, the car that now looks like a little Matchbox model down on the road. About an hour later we start filming. The wind has picked up, and whatever I say comes straight out of my mouth and is probably in Scarborough a couple of minutes later. Then it's time for the tyre. We haven't checked with the National Trust, who own this stretch of land, or the RSPB, who protect the twites and plovers that supposedly nest on the moor, or the police, who probably have a law against rolling heavy objects in the direction of a public highway. Neither have we warned the solitary hiker, who, as ill fortune would have it, strolls into view on the lower slope just as I kick the tyre over the lip of the hill.

'Something there is that doesn't love a wall,' wrote Robert Frost. About walls. If he thought walls were unappreciated he should have tried tyres. Nothing loves a tyre – the devil is in them, steering them into misfortune and ill consequence, egging them on into trouble. Keith is unaware of this, being halfway down the slope with the big eye of the camera looking back towards me. Rather heroically, I think, he keeps his finger on the trigger till the last moment, then dives for the ground as the tyre lunges at his throat. Having missed him, but now travelling with substantial momentum and apparent determination, the tyre uses the camber of the hillside to adjust its course towards its new target. The hiker, ignorant of any danger, has mounted a small ridge above a scree slope, and in the mind of the tyre is a sitting duck. What would that be like, to escape the city, to leave the traffic behind and head for the empty hills, only to be hit by a tyre? How would it sound in court, or at the inquest? The traces of black rubber are on my hands. The tread leads back to my feet. Collision seems inevitable. I look towards Keith, but Keith is checking the camera. I look for the media studies student but she is on the phone. And I think about shouting, but before I do, an alternative plan enters my mind, which is to leg it. I drop to the ground and perform a strangely accomplished commando roll away from the rim of the summit. Out of view, I remain on the ground on my back, staring into the sky, listening for screams or sirens. After several minutes I crawl back to the edge of the hill, part a clump of tussock grass and peer down the slope. The rambler is nowhere to be seen. About a quarter of a mile away, the media studies student is standing with one foot on the innocent, inert tyre, eating a banana. Keith is about twenty feet away, walking towards me. 'It was good,' he says, 'but I'd like to try it once more.'

*

For the last two years I've been translating the classic medieval poem *Sir Gawain and the Green Knight*. It's an epic tale of daring and temptation, and verses 53 and 54 are not for the faint-hearted. For while Gawain 'made myry al day, til the mone rysed' (i.e. lounged in the castle, flirting with the ladies), the lord of the land was out gralloching. I hadn't come across that term until I started looking into the art of deer-butchery, with which the *Gawain* poet was clearly well acquainted. Towards the end of a rip-roaring hunting scene, and with no little relish, he describes the whole process, from the hacking off of the heads to the slicing open of the stomachs. No portion of the animal seems to escape the hunter's knife or the poet's eye, with some of the more grisly portions being guzzled by the dogs or tossed into the woods for the crows. But as full and frank as these passages are, I figured that only by seeing the real thing would I get a true sense of what was actually taking place. And if watching a deer being skinned is part and parcel of the poet's daily life, then Keith must come too. So with the tyre locked in the boot of the car like a kidnap victim, we head towards a farm on the Yorkshire–Lancashire border. And no ordinary farm, at least by Pennine standards, because the shapes in the fields above us are not those of cows and horses but the less familiar outlines of elk and deer. A llama peers over a dry-stone wall, sniffs the air, then returns to its ruminating. The farmer tells me he's had bison here as well, and other creatures of the prairies and steppes. In his kitchen, we sit down for a cup of tea among the mounted heads of many a horned beast. On the windowsill a stuffed ferret bares the vicious white needles of its teeth.

'How can you tell a weasel from a stoat?' I ask him.

'Go on.'

'Well, weasels are weaselly recognized, but stoats are stoatally different.'

'So what is it you do for a living?'

A bit later, I'm standing around in the yard in a pair of borrowed wellies when the single crack of a high-velocity rifle – like a wooden ruler snapped across the knee – echoes between the walls of the outbuildings. A couple of minutes later the farmer comes skidding around the corner with his gun on his shoulder and a small, dead deer lolling over the back end of his quad bike. The slaughterhouse is a tall shed with a concrete floor. The farmer and his assistant, both wearing bloodstained white smocks like two mad dentists from a slasher movie, hoist the deer in a kind of metal cradle and in just a few seconds of mesmerizing knife-work have removed its hide entirely. Then with a single cut from throat to groin they open it up. It's kind of horrible, kind of beautiful. I've never been very good with meat and blood, but the revulsion is tempered by the speed and expertise of the slaughtermen – it's too precise to be disgusting. The only time I feel last night's supper rising towards my mouth is when he slices open the gut and out drops a big dollop of steaming, almost luminous green grass. The farmer gives me a running commentary on all the bits and pieces, especially those which crop up in the poem, such as the knot, the chine and the slot. The only term he can't help me with is 'numbles'.

'No, never 'eard of it,' he says. Then adds, 'But I got numbled last night in the pub. Well fuckin' numbled.'

It's all over in a few minutes. The meat is bagged up ready to go, and the innards are dumped in a skip. It was a fallow deer, I think. Now very fallow indeed, it occurs to me, as it peeps over the rim of a blue plastic bin, the pretty head still attached to the empty cloak of its skin. Keith lowers the camera. Invited back into the house, we scrub our hands in the sink while the farmer's wife drops a knob of butter into a frying pan, followed by a couple of thick, bloody venison steaks. With a mouthful of deer, I agree with the farmer that it's a tasty meat, but not necessarily something I'd choose for breakfast.

I don't find it very easy being followed around by a cameraman, and I don't suppose Keith finds it easy making a film of a poet translating a poem written in 1400. Me sitting on my backside crunching through dictionaries of Middle English is hardly a feast of visual entertainment. If Keith had been around a couple of years ago, when I first tried to see the original manuscript of *Gawain*, he might have been witness to something mildly amusing and worthy of broadcast. But he wasn't, unfortunately, so unless the incident was recorded on CCTV, it is now entirely a matter of memory. And according to my memory, it went something like this. I'm in the reading room of the British Library, and the lady on the desk seems torn between taking me seriously and sliding her hand towards the panic button. Behind me, a couple of dozen eggheads, poring over ancients maps and documents, have overheard my outrageous request and have raised their eyes to just over the rim of their spectacles. The lady says, 'You do realize it is one of our most priceless possessions?'

It isn't a particularly cold day in London, though when I left Yorkshire at 7 a.m. there was frost on the pavement. This is why I am wearing a heavy-duty parka and a pair of big boots, and why I am sweating. I've never been in the British Library before, and with my new membership card laminated less than an hour ago, I'm beginning to wish that was still the case. At this stage, the mature and responsible course of action would be to say something like, 'My name is Simon Armitage, I'm a published poet, and I've been commissioned to translate the poem for my publishers, Faber & Faber in this country and Norton in the US.' Who knows, she might even have heard of me. But instead of rising to the task, I have entered what is often referred to in our house as Alan Bennett mode, characterized by the outward demonstration of inadequacy and unworthiness when standing before the edifices of the Establishment. So instead of speaking, I just sweat some more, and to the lady on the desk, on the verge of a diagnosis, this is the clinching evidence. I am a nutter. Not out of prejudice but out of fear, she says, 'There aren't many pictures in it.'

Although my back is turned to them, I'm pretty certain that the learned scholars behind me have now given up any pretence of work and are watching this little cameo scene with great amusement. They have pushed aside the Magna Carta, or the Mappa Mundi, or the original copy of the Holy Bible written by God himself, and they are sniggering.

'There are twelve illustrations,' I tell the lady, attempting to demonstrate some knowledge of the manuscript, but then the Alan Bennett in me tells me I might have been a little abrupt, so I qualify this with, 'I think.'

The lady says, 'We have some nice postcards of them. You can buy them downstairs in the gift shop.' Ten minutes later I'm on a bench at King's Cross waiting for the next train north. From a little paper bag I pull out six or seven postcards. The lady was right. They are indeed very nice, and beautifully reproduced.

We want a lot of music in the film, so as well as putting together a soundtrack of my favourite Yorkshire bands, I suggest we shoot a scene at Vinyl Tap, the online record shop run by my mate Tony from a warehouse just outside Huddersfield. The offices are upstairs. Downstairs it's an Aladdin's cave of albums and CDs, hundreds of thousands of them stacked on trestle tables. Five years ago, vinyl was just for hi-fi enthusiasts and Japanese record collectors with more money than taste, but these days everyone is at it. Keith buys a Utah Saints single, featuring himself on drums, which is either a very sad or a very cool thing to do. With the camera rolling, I pull out the Crispy Ambulance 12-inch I've been after for twenty-five years. Crispy Ambulance were not an easy band to like. The name, for one thing – not something you'd want tattooing on your chest, almost as daft as Prefab Sprout – and their first album, *The Plateau Phase*, gave me a headache. But their tour de force, 'The Presence', occupying an entire side of the *Live on a Hot August Night* EP, is thirteen minutes of contained wonder, a kind of post-punk, anti-matter alternative to Lynyrd Skynyrd's gaudy and indulgent 'Free Bird', a repeat offender on *The Old Grey Whistle*

Test at the time. I never owned 'The Presence', but my mate Rob did, and he lent it to me for a couple of months in the summer before I went off to college. The summer before everything changed. Mum and Dad were on holiday and for the first time I'd been trusted to stay in the house on my own. I had a Fidelity belt-drive record player, bought with the non-taxable earnings from my summer job as a lathe operator at a local engineering company. They made motors for washing machines and Harrier jump jets. As a precaution, I was put on the washing machine side of production. For eight hours a day I loaded shiny metal rods – like spindles – on to a precision lathe, and pressed a button. As the rod rotated at great speed, a diamond-tipped cutting tool passed across its surface, reducing it to the required diameter. The machine also threw out a spray of coolant, a milky-looking mixture of oil and water, that left me with a white stripe from the top of my trousers to the collar of my shirt. When I became particularly proficient they put me in charge of a second lathe, right behind me, which produced a similar stripe from the nape of my neck to the base of my spine. I'd get home late in the evening, bearing the strange markings and smelling of engineering, but I didn't care. I had beer in the fridge – legally bought – and money in my pocket – honestly earned. I carried the Fidelity into the garden and plugged it into the extension cable from the lawnmower. I put one speaker in the gnarled arms of the lilac tree and one on the dried-up bird bath. It was hot, August, and almost night, and for the next thirteen minutes I had the soundtrack to go with it. Then I'd lift the arm – the awkward, plastic arm with the little crucifix of the stylus tight in its grip – and play it once more. And maybe that's why I've bought this record a quarter of a century later. So for quarter of an hour, I can have it over and over again.

On the Road 4

November 2005. I'm giving poetry readings in the USA – North Carolina, Georgia, South Carolina. It's difficult to know how the poems will sound or if they will translate: the audience are English-speaking, obviously, but many of the poems are based in one particular village, looking out of one particular window, and at the time they were written had no ambitions beyond the visible horizon. Will the Yorkshire Moors and the motorway between Leeds and Manchester hold much meaning or interest for an audience in the American South? I start with a poem called 'The Shout', which in my own mind at least has become something of a signature tune. It's a small, set-piece poem that says a lot about the place I'm from, the things I write about and my poetic style. It's like the staple in the middle of a Philips' Planisphere, holding it all in place. The further I am away from home, the more prominence I tend to give it, and tonight it's top of the bill. I also spend a long time setting the poem up, even though the piece itself is less than half a page long, takes about thirty seconds to read and is perfectly self-explanatory to all but the most comatose audience. Explaining individual poems can be an unedifying business. Start describing how and why they were made, or worse, what they mean, and you reach a point where the poem seems to hold no value or intrigue whatsoever.

But at a reading, introductions to poems are not only useful, they're a necessary form of relief, giving the audience permission to relax before tuning in to the next piece.

At the junior school in the village where I grew up, we had an eccentric science teacher and virtually no equipment, which was a perplexing combination. He didn't set us experiments – they were more like little missions – and one day he asked me and another boy to go outside and not come back until we'd measured the size of the human voice. Without equipment. Between us we came up with a plan: the other boy would walk away, and every once in a while he'd turn around and shout. If I heard him I'd raise my arm. Eventually there would come a point where his bellowing would be inaudible to me. Then we'd pace out the distance between us, and that measurement would be the size of the human voice. So off he went. Unfortunately, local topography meant that after a while he simply disappeared out of sight. Off the map. Over the edge, into some dark place, such as Lancashire. Thirty years later I was told that the boy, whose name and whose features I can't even remember, had shot himself through the roof of his mouth somewhere on the far side of the world. So the poem trades on the idea that no sound ever completely dies, and that every utterance ever made is still resonating out through the cosmos at some infinitely low level. There's one small geographical reference in the poem that will be meaningless to all but a few and is worth a quick mention. Most of the houses in the village of Marsden are down in the bottom of a natural geographical bowl, with one notable exception. Fretwell's Farm sits on top of Binn

Moor, way above every other dwelling. The apex of the roof and the chimney pot are just about visible from the picture window of my mum and dad's front room. And at night, so is the light in the farmyard. The Fretwells don't live there any more – in fact the true name of the farmstead is Acre Head. But when I was a boy, and it got dark, and the black of the night sky and the black of the moor merged into one unbroken backcloth of darkness, that light used to shine like a star, and people talked about Fretwell's Farm as if it were a constellation – something you could steer a course by if you were lost and heading for home. Just below the horizon, all on their own, there are three gnarled old trees, their trunks bent to the east by the force of the wind that screams around the edge of the hill. And beneath the trees there's a pile of old stones that was once another farm called the Blue Pig. When the Blue Pig caught fire, sixty years ago maybe, the son of the house ran down to the fire station in his bare feet, but by the time the local fire brigade, including my grandfather, had struggled up the hill with buckets and hoses, the roof had collapsed and the father had burnt to death. One version of the story says he'd gone back into the house to get his money. Like I said, all utterances, even whispers, never completely disappear. I've sometimes wondered if the bucket of water my granddad carried up the hill was the same bucket he used to bring the head of a German pilot back down to the village after an enemy bomber had crashed on the moor during the war.

Another poem I tend to read and introduce is called 'The Winner'. It was written as a fairly earnest response to a real and worrying situation. When I was in my late twenties, and after a series of excruciating back problems that forced me to hang up my football boots and sell my stumping gloves, I was diagnosed as suffering from ankylosing spondylitis, a degenerative and at that time untreatable condition. I was told the vertebrae of my spine were slowly but surely knitting together, and that eventually I would develop a pronounced and painful hunch before seizing up altogether. A well-wisher bought me a year's subscription to the National Ankylosing Spondylitis Society magazine, whose descent-of-man cartoon logo depicted an AS sufferer in various degrees of spinal curvature. As a worst-case scenario, if the condition kept on progressing at the same rate I might have to choose a permanent position to spend the rest of my life in, because I was fossilizing, basically. At first I wept. I was very interested in astronomy at the time, and the prospect of staring at my shoes for the rest of my days rather than the stars was almost too much to bear. But after a few months I had a change of mood, and got very bloody-minded about the whole thing. Quite simply, I decided I wasn't prepared to end up looking like something hanging from Mother Shipton's Cave or one of those trees at the Blue Pig. Surrender was not an option. Flexibility was everything – I'd keep twisting and bending and touching my toes, no matter how much it hurt. And during daydreams, I fantasized about imitating the ultimate martyr: if I did have to choose a position to spend the rest of my life in, it wouldn't be something benign like the sitting or the foetal position. Instead, I'd stand up straight with my arms out and adopt the shape of Christ on the Cross. (This would have been completely impractical, of course: we had a small Ford Fiesta at the time – either they would have had to load me through the hatchback or I would have had to stand in the sunroof and go down the street like crucified Noddy in his little motor. Church would also have been embarrassing, especially at Easter.) I read all the books and tried all the advice. I even went to see a very strange Frenchman in Brighton who told me the only way to get better was to eat all my daily meals before noon. That way, my body wouldn't have to digest any food at night and would heal itself while I slept. I could certainly see the logic of this, but over a microwaved bacon sandwich and a can of Stella on the last train back to Huddersfield that evening, I realized my lifestyle just wasn't suited to this form of treatment. So instead I wrote poems. Dozens of them, all wallowing in the misery of the illness or poking fun at it. And eventually it disappeared. There are people who think of poetry as a form of therapy, or argue that poetry can help generate and release certain chemicals necessary to the mending of a broken spirit or a broken body. I'm not sure about that. But certainly in my case something happened. It was as if I'd aimed all my creative energy towards the illness, and scared it away. Poetry can certainly have that effect – maybe I'd bored it into submission. In 'The Winner' I describe a person whose bodily malfunctions have reached ludicrous proportions, but despite losing almost every limb and function, the person in question still manages to take the life-saving test at his local swimming baths and complete the Lyke Wake Walk. The Lyke Wake Walk is a forty-or-so-mile trek across the North York Moors that follows the path once taken by monks as they processed

THE LYKE WAKE CLUB

Condolences on your crossing!

Simon Armitage

Date 28th May, 1978.   Time 17hr. 50mins.

THE CHIEF DIRGER,
POTTO HILL, SWAINBY,
NORTHALLERTON.

towards the coast to bury their dead at sea. Complete it in less than twenty-four hours and the Chief Dirger sends you a black lapel badge in the shape of a coffin. And the life-saving test, as far as I remember, involved turning up at the swimming baths at some point in your school swimming career wearing only your pyjamas, then rescuing a rubber weight from the deep end. Without explanation. In some of my more heroic fantasies in later life, some poor soul has dropped their rubber weight into the murky depths of the Leeds–Liverpool canal, but fear not, for help is close at hand because, as luck would have it, yours truly just happens to be sauntering along the tow-path in his winceyette nightwear, and is fully qualified to dive in and retrieve it.

With the reading 'tour' over I'm catching the first plane home. So Friday night goes past in a blur of laughable meals and a not-so-funny zom-com film over the Atlantic. In the pod of the aeroplane toilet (a constriction in which even Harry Houdini would have struggled to unbutton himself) I examine my blotchy, travel-worn face in the metal mirror. I look kind of . . . deceased. On a positive note, the dark shadows around the eyes have concealed the fortnight-old purple bruise occasioned by the Tudge's vigorous approach to crazy golf. I find myself thinking that however enriching Anglo–US poetics might be, until the invention of the matter transporter, the process of transatlantic air travel will always be something like a steel putter across the temples. Morning is a warm, moist flannel somewhere above Dublin.

By mid-afternoon on Saturday I'm starring in my own zom-com, stumbling between rooms and banging into furniture, desperate for sleep. Only the thought of tonight's bonfire keeps me going – light at the end of the tunnel. The Tudge explains the legend of Guy Fawkes: 'He was in the colourful church, and he was ganging under the house next door to King James who was the boss of the dull church. But then they caught him and got him dead with a rope around his neck and it was all happy again.' There's something beautifully home-made and amateurish about the traditional British bonfire, and tonight's turns out to be no exception: a makeshift pyre; toffee and pie in a neighbour's garage; bottles of beer jemmied open with a penknife; conspiratorial silhouettes up in the field, ducking from the sideways strafing of misaligned Roman candles. Sunday is Sunday. It tipples down. Tradition dictates we gorge on roasted meat and boiled vegetables, and we happily oblige. We pull on our wellies and make a tour of the pile of smouldering charcoal, still alight at the core despite the weather. It's an undemonstrative aftermath. An English volcano. A low-lying but deep-seated, unquenched and seemingly inexhaustible flame.

The Long-range Forecast

♪

Some boy brushes your elbow and spills the drinks –
down comes the red mist.
Some boy offers a handshake that looks like a fist –
down comes the red mist.
Some boy thinks that he's so funny and so clever
but he's taking the piss.
High pressure. Stormy weather.
Down comes the red mist. Down comes the red mist.

This is the long-range forecast:
peacocks poncing around in the courtyard.

This is the long-range forecast:
two visits a month and four phonecards.

This is the long-range forecast:
Now That's What I Call Mind-Numbing Boredom
    on all formats.

This is the long-range forecast:
peacocks baring their fundaments before breakfast.

This is the long-range forecast:
two hundred boys in a marathon wank-fest.

This is the long-range forecast:
three hundred and sixty-five ways of eating a Mars bar.

This is the long-range forecast:
two-fifty a week but no council tax.

This is the long-range forecast:
peacocks strutting about like bastards.

This is the long-range forecast:
car-crime nobodies versus the drug-running all-stars.

This is the long-range forecast:
a last supper of Creme Eggs and Liquorice Allsorts.

This is the long-range forecast:
a future of pool cues and table tennis bats.

This is the long-range forecast:
peacocks bigging it up in the car park.

This is the long-range forecast:
screws with clipboards marking the scorecards.

This is the long-range forecast:
a windowsill full of family photographs.

This is the long-range forecast:
a peacock outside doing the royal walkabout.

Gig

This is the long-range forecast:
life burning away into smoke and fag-ash.

This is the long-range forecast:
the sound of your own thoughts at full-blast.

This is the long-range forecast:
peacocks having it large on the flat roofs.

This is the long-range forecast:
two visits a month and four phonecards.

This is the long-range forecast:
down comes the red mist, put on your fog-lamps.

♫

Sung by Darbon in the film *Feltham Sings* (Century Films/ Channel 4, 2002).

Royal Festival Hall
8 November 2005

From the breeze-block green room at the back of the theatre, eight or nine of us take our turn to shuffle out on to the stage, read a few poems, then sink into a seat in the audience. The last poet of the night is Michael Donaghy. From nowhere he enters the beam of the spotlight, approaches the microphone, and for the next ten minutes gives a flawless and mesmerizing recitation of his long poem 'Black Ice and Rain'. Which is all very bewildering, because Mike is dead.

Michael Donaghy was as much a musician as he was a poet. His poems were exercises in melodic structure, his ear for rhythm and the lyric timing of a line was faultless, and in his opening lines – those words that announce the poem's entry into the world – he was pitch-perfect. A born entertainer, he knew his poems by heart, and recited them with no need of a book as either a prompt or a prop, but never crossed the line into theatricality, or sold himself short for the sake of an immediate reaction or an easy response. There was also something of the trickster about Mike, a magician drawing lines out of thin air, pulling metaphors out of a hat, sawing reality in half. He was not a performance poet but a performer of his poems, and being present at one of his readings was like witnessing pop-up 3D versions of the written work. There was a morbid irony to the timing of his death. The Next Generation of poets had just been announced, replacing the New Generation, which included Mike among its ranks. It was typical of his sense of humour and human dignity that he should interpret the suggestion to move aside so literally.

Mike's work exemplified the new buoyancy in poetry during the late eighties/early nineties. He was a communicator who loved an audience. On the page, with one choice phrase, he could bridge the worlds of philosophy and popular culture. I even heard that he liked to write standing at a lectern, as if the final delivery of the poem was never far from his mind. In a room, he couldn't be ignored. He never stopped laughing and he never shut up, except to put his tin whistle in his mouth. Full of intellectual fizz, from his computer he spied, sabotaged and waged war on the enemy, righting poetic wrongs in far-flung corners of the World Wide Web, fighting against those who would do his chosen art a disservice. But my abiding memory of him isn't really a literary one. It's Mike at 3 a.m. on the dance floor in a smoky nightclub in Seville, after a reading, high as a kite, throwing some mad shapes.

In the weeks before this event, wondering which of his poems I should read, I'd pulled a copy of one his books from the shelf and found a postcard inside it. On one side was a picture of John Donne. On the other he'd written, 'Dear Folks, I'm sending you my book as a wedding present because it's cheaper than a blender and easier to fit in the envelope.' And to me this was Michael in a nutshell. One half modern metaphysicist, one half Tommy Cooper.

Watching his projected apparition on the screen in front of us is to witness that phenomenon again. Very few of us in the packed auditorium of the Purcell Room, here for this celebration of his work and commemoration of his life, knew this film footage of Michael existed, let alone that it would be screened. Very few of us ever imagined we'd see him in action again. The gesticulation. The facial mannerisms. The eye movement and the body language. The verbal sleight of hand. Shaving with a blunt razor about an hour before the reading I'd nicked myself on the corner of my lip and turned up at the venue wearing a not very fetching blob of tissue glued to my face with congealed plasma. About halfway through the screening of Mike's poem, hypnotized and not a little shocked by the image in front of me, I realize I've been absent-mindedly jabbing away at the cut with my fingernail and have opened up the wound again. The film ends and Mike's ghost dissolves into the blackness. The living poets pull themselves out of their seats, climb the three or four steps to the stage, forage for an opening in the closed curtains and return to the dressing room. I'm embarrassed, because most of the gathering now comforting each other or shaking hands or reaching for the bottle were closer to Mike than me, or had known him for longer. But in the bathroom, in a wall-sized mirror framed by light bulbs, I am literally blood, sweat and tears.

The Mark Radcliffe Show
BBC Radio 2
3 January 2006

I was once a Radio 1 DJ for two hours – it says so on my CV. I'd been popping in to the *Mark Radcliffe Show* at Manchester's 'Palace of Glittering Delights' every two or three weeks, then hosted it on one occasion, on National Poetry Day, while Mark was away on holiday. I say hosted – all the spontaneous intros and rapid-fire monologues were pre-recorded, and all the technical business such as playing in jingles and cueing up CDs was done from behind a wall of glass by people who actually knew which buttons to press. All I had to do was chip in with the odd comment, explore a few connections between the art of poetry and the art of lyric writing, and interview a couple of pop stars. Damon Albarn had just flown back from the States. He was sulky and quiet in the cubicle, but brightened up in the studio. With his feet on the table and the soles of his Doc Martens staring me in the face, he talked about writing the words for the *Parklife* album, and in particular the extended metaphor that is 'This is a Low'. He was thoughtful, generous, disturbingly pretty and of course cool beyond anything I'd ever encountered. In terms of degrees Fahrenheit, Elizabeth Fraser of the Cocteau Twins was not cool at all, but hot and bothered. Or at least very flustered. She'd brought several notebooks into the studio full of scribbled phrases and weird hiero-glyphics. I wanted her to say how the words in front of her became the words to her songs, and was especially curious about her guest vocal on the Felt song 'Primitive Painters', on which she seems to be singing, 'You should see my trail of disgrace.' But I was asking the impossible. I was asking her to describe the ineffable. I put it to her that she used her voice as an instrument, and she replied with silence. I felt like a detective sergeant in an interview room with the tape running: 'At this point the suspect smiles, shrugs her shoulders and nods her head.' I compli-mented her on her handwriting, she gathered up her books of spells and we moved on.

I carried on making guest appearances with Mark and Lard until they 'got the call' and moved to a daytime slot, where poetry couldn't coexist with Barry White impersonations, wall-to-wall knob gags and chart hits. But several years later and several years older, Mark was back on the graveyard shift, this time on Radio 2, and this time without his sidekick, now working as a presenter in his own right and known by his grown-up name, Marc Riley. So suddenly I'm back in a studio, reading poems on a national music network. In many ways, it's the dream gig. During the spring, I finish teaching at the university just along the road at about 9 p.m. and wander slowly towards town with a kebab or a pizza slice. Or in the autumn, I leave home at half-time of whichever football fixture is taking place that night and arrive at the fortified side-gates of Broadcasting House just before the final whistle. And sometimes I make a few notes on a Post-it, things I might talk about (I'm supposed to be their literary correspondent, I seem to remember), though it rarely goes to plan. Tonight, three days into the New Year, we end up talking about Christmas rituals, and I suggest that within families, many such habits or traditions take the form of games. Not board games or video games, but old-fashioned games, handed down through the generations, often requiring little more than a pen and paper and sometimes not even that. I have no evidence for this theory other than the game-playing that takes place within my family over the festive period, and which I realized this year has become a kind of forty-eight-hour residential application for Mensa. No sooner is the dishwasher loaded than the first quiz sheet is being distributed, usually by my sister, and usually comprising the faces of unnamed celebrities scissored from the Christmas edition of the *Radio Times* and Pritt-stuck to a sheet of A4. The task is one of simple identification, but after a Buck's Fizz breakfast, a bottle of red at the table, a Christmas pudding fuming with brandy, a small glass of 'something from the cupboard' and a couple of chocolate liqueurs, it's surprising how much the powers of recognition are blunted. In my case, this results in Mr Blobby being mistaken for Barbapapa and Jonathan Ross for Jennie Bond. Next comes Sweet Bingo, an apparently benign and innocuous game in which tubes of Smarties, bags of wine gums and the obligatory Chocolate Orange are presented to the holders of numbered tickets as the numbers are called, bingo-style, by our unflappable hostess, Auntie Betty. However, new animosities are aroused and old enmities awoken once the stockpile of confectionery has vanished, because it's at this point that winning ticket holders earn the right to retrieve prizes from other members of the family. During this period of mayhem and shamelessness, Curly Wurlies and packets of Love Hearts are gleefully commandeered by aunts and uncles, Jelly Tots are prised from the clutches of weeping infants by marauding adults, and a large bag of liquorice – the most coveted item of all – changes hands several times before landing in the sweaty mitts of the unbearable, gloating victor. The fact that bowls of chocolate brazils and creamy toffees are freely available on every work surface in the house appears to make no difference to the participants of this game, whose motivation is not to posses but to deprive.

Yet the unpleasantness of Sweet Bingo is but a trifle compared to the tribal feuding and internecine acrimony that is Town and Country, truly the gold-ribbon event of the Armitage Christmas Olympics, usually kicking off at about 8.30 p.m. on Boxing Day. The rules are clear enough. Players are divided into teams. Each player chooses a category – towns, countries, musical instruments, films, whatever – then a letter is picked at random from the page of a book, and each team has ten or so minutes to think of something in each category beginning with the given letter. One point for an answer shared by another team, two points for an answer that is unique. On paper it sounds simple, but in practice it's a riot. This year's unrest begins in the category of Rivers, a usually uncontroversial and quiet passage of play. The letter in question is S, and while all other teams are making do with the Severn and the Stour, my own team, of which I am the captain, naturally, comes up with the river Styx – an answer that speaks of both imaginative power and intellectual prowess, and is clearly the thinking of a genius. So I'm utterly flabbergasted when Styx is referred to the 'panel', an arbitrarily appointed body of individuals consisting of an auntie from Greenock and my thirteen-year-old niece. And when Styx is rejected, in what seems to me at that moment to be the biggest competitive injustice of all time, I'm incensed. Suddenly I'm Mike Gatting remonstrating with umpire Shakoor Rana. Then I'm a petulant Tory front-bencher, rising from his seat and waving his paper. Speedy Sue pulls me back down by the lap of my shirt, but I stand up again. Now I'm a barrister, citing case histories from previous years, pointing out that the acceptance of Noddy as a TV Personality during Christmas 1997 set a precedent for the use of myth and fiction within essentially factual categories. But when my mother-in-law – who in over a decade of impeccable mother-in-lawing has never disbelieved or contradicted a single word I have uttered – casts doubt on the legitimacy of the answer, I'm screwed. I can't work with these people. I can't carry on in these conditions. I make an undignified retreat to the kitchen, but return in less than a minute with a large gin in my hand and revenge on my mind.

A number of people text or email the *Mark Radcliffe Show* with their own stories of Christmas games and the ultra-competitiveness they seem to induce, before we move on to our second topic for the night: the New Year's Eve disco. Back in the analogue era, compilations of favourite songs by various artists were lovingly, laboriously and illegally copied from vinyl to cassette tape. But since the dawn of the digital age, something called the playlist has replaced the compilation tape. Playlists are effortless, legitimate and available to all but the most begrudging Luddite or dunderhead technophobe. And the record collection has been replaced by the iPod.

In one sense, this is the revolution we've all been waiting for. What could be better than carrying every tune you've ever enjoyed in your top pocket? What could be more irresistible than containing your entire musical taste within an object whose size is often likened to that of a cigarette packet, or to a non-smoker like myself, a small slab of Kendal Mint Cake or *The Observer's Book of Birds*? And what could be more exciting than editing 10,000 tracks into categories and track listings of your very own choosing? On the other hand, since the arrival of the iPod, everyone is a DJ. And as the self-appointed MC of the New Year's Eve disco, the idea that I might be challenged for control of the docking station is a troubling thought. What if they're bigger and stronger than me? What if they play better music?

If you've ever wondered why people make New Year's resolutions, think for a moment about the context in which these lifestyle pledges occur. Roughly a week before the end of the old year, having almost bankrupted themselves on consumer durables, people start to drink, beginning around the evening of 24 December. The drinks can be quite alien to their system. Snowball. Rum punch. Something involving Baileys and another liquid with which it refuses to blend – motor oil, possibly. It is also around this time that they begin to eat. Again, it's not the stuff the average metabolism has come to expect. They eat chestnuts. They eat capon. They digest gluttonous quantities of rich, savoury food, then tarmac over it with layers of tiramisu and plum duff. Loaded and bloated, they retire to the living room to laugh and argue, leaving half-devoured carcasses and other perishables to fester and ripen in the overheated kitchen. For three more days they feast on these putrefying and rancid leftovers. The cheeseboard in particular, never once covered let alone refrigerated, is a Petri dish of bacterial activity. Then people stay up late watching their new DVDs and rise early with their excitable children. This pattern continues until the last day of the year, when they begin the process all over again, but this time with real purpose and renewed vigour. This time the clock is against them. They drink in the afternoon and in the evening they feast. Pâté. Anchovies. Stinking Bishop. On the point of midnight, uncoordinated and incoherent, they introduce into their systems more alcohol, this time with bubbles in it, just to make absolutely sure, then stumble outside to grope around in the boot of the car or the back of the garage for that final ingredient, without which the impending catastrophe of New Year's Eve would be incomplete: gunpowder. And it is in this context – exhausted, poisoned and, in all probability, seriously burnt – that resolutions are made. These are the circumstances in which the individual makes a solemn pledge to society, the mind swears an oath to the body, and owners apologize to their dogs.

As all this is taking place, my final resolution of the *old* year is to bring the incoherent and uncoordinated to the dance floor. And as I see it, with about thirty friends gathered in a rented farmhouse above Heptonstall, there are four crucial choices to be made: what to play first, what to play last, which record represents the highpoint of the whole night, and when to play Abba. In fact that final decision is made for me by my iPod's random shuffle feature, which selects 'Dancing Queen' as the second song of the evening (clearly too early), right after the opener, Sister Sledge's 'Lost in Music'. The Stone Roses' 'I Am The Resurrection' is the undisputed moment of glory, even amongst those who haven't heard it before, and is perfectly positioned at five minutes to midnight. Other hotspots include 'She Sells Sanctuary', during which a small, local mosh pit develops, taking out a couple of chairs and a table lamp, and The Fall's 'Mr Pharmacist', or 'Mr Armitage' as the chant becomes. But finally, and most intriguing of all, is the Smiths' 'Reel Around the Fountain', which invokes amongst the nine or ten of us still on our feet a spectacle of such weirdness that I hesitate to describe it. Imagine morris dancing meets *The Wicker Man* meets amateur rugby union, and you're about half-way there. One moment we're holding hands in a circle, the next we're on our knees worshipping some invisible presence, and finally we fall in a collapsed scrummage, a big human pile, with blood injuries and temporary respiratory problems the inevitable consequence. To add to the confusion, we've been projecting Series One of *I'm Alan Partridge* on to the ceiling above us – a ten-foot-long, elongated Steve Coogan in a leather posing pouch, splashed across the beams and plaster of a seventeenth-century dwelling in a dark Pennine valley. In those circumstances, it is perhaps understandable that so many people should simultaneously and collectively lose their balance.

★

The *Mark Radcliffe Show* ends at midnight; half an hour later I've escaped Manchester and I'm heading over Saddleworth Moor, as usual in the fog. The road, not busy at the best of times, is deserted. At the junction with Wessenden Head Road it's not unusual to see a hare – the same one? – either bundling off into the blackness like a rubber band unwinding itself, or just sitting there, trying to outstare the headlights. Tonight he's here again, but lifeless and buckled, clipped by a bumper or a tyre. In daylight I might have pulled up, checked him over or put him out of his misery. But on Saddleworth Moor at 12.45 a.m. in the fog, you don't get out of your vehicle. You look straight ahead, you lock your arms at ten to two on the steering wheel, and you drive. And if you're listening to the iPod through the car stereo and the shuffle feature chooses 'Suffer Little Children', you skip to the next track, or you yank out the wire.

So Imagine My Disappointment When . . .

iTunes offers a feature called Just For You. Based on the music you've purchased from their Music Store, it suggests a top ten of other songs you'd almost certainly enjoy. This morning at no. 6: 'Too Shy' by Kajagoogoo.

Arctic Monkeys
Leeds University
1 February 2006

Being a sucker for skinny white northerners singing about riot vans and opportunist theft, and given that Arctic Monkeys are this week's biggest band in the universe, this gig is a must. Like half a million others, I bought the album on the day it came out, and it's a winning mix of honest guitar riffs, *Shameless*-esque stories, and tunes you can whistle and sing. It's also about love. *Whatever People Say I Am, That's What I'm Not* is a day in the life of the nothing-to-do generation, from the spliff-for-breakfast mid-morning to the pissed-up end of the night, via happy hour, last orders and the scuffle in the taxi queue. In the hands of a less gifted lyricist, this would just be another mouthy mither from Peasant Crescent. But through engaging narratives and subtle half-rhymes, and in an undiluted republic-of-South-Yorkshire accent, comes a plea for romance. It can't be easy, looking for love in a wind-tunnel shopping precinct when everyone else is looking for pharmaceuticals or a knife fight, but love is what Alex Turner seems to be asking for, and I'm happy to oblige.

I'm also happy that Arctic Monkeys are from Sheffield. Musically speaking, I've always had a soft spot for the city, dating back to the first Comsat Angels album. I only saw them play once, at Futurama, a kind of indoor Glastonbury in Leeds city centre. The event took place over a weekend; if the security guards were feeling gener-ous or lazy they'd let you bed down for the night at the back of the venue on the concrete floor among the glue sniffers and broken bottles. If they were doing their job, you'd have to thumb it back to Huddersfield or sleep in a subway, then return in the morning. The venue, the Queens Hall, was an echoey, soulless hangar of a place, but at least it never rained, unless you count the evening the Bay City Rollers made their ill-advised headline appearance, when it rained bottles and cans. To play Futurama, the Comsat Angels would have travelled all of thirty miles up the M1, the motorway that – I've always presumed – features on the cover of *Waiting for a Miracle*. It's a terse, slightly blurred and tilted photograph, prob-ably taken from a car window, with the tarmac and sodium of the carriageway in the foreground and the post-industrial Pompeii of pre-Meadowhall Sheffield behind it. Through a gash in the clouds, the humped incline of a dark moor is just visible in the far background. As a snapshot, it says everything about the music inside the sleeve. I bought my own copy from Bostock Records in Huddersfield, the knock-off record shop next to the cut-price butcher's. Even now, if it enters my nostrils, the smell of scraggy meat and cheap pies takes me straight back to that shop, and those Saturday afternoons spent walking my fingers through the racks of imported albums, manfully resisting Eric Clapton's *Slowhand* or the omni-potent *Tubular Bells*. The Comsat Angels' second album, *Sleep No More*, was released the month I left Yorkshire to begin life as a homesick student at Portsmouth Poly. With the sparseness of the early songs now pared down even further, and with a deadpan, distant drumbeat apparently performed outside the lift shaft of Polydor studios and recorded from three or four floors away, it is their finest hour. The winter of '81 was intensely cold, with railway workers having to light fires under their engines to thaw out the diesel. A week before Christmas, after a 250-mile journey of broken-down buses, thumbed lifts and missed connections, I stumbled from the guard's van of a slowed-down train on to Marsden station. I'd made it home. It was about eleven at night. Feathery snowflakes were drifting noiselessly and vertically into the dome of the valley, and the village looked like the perfect model of itself, housed inside a souvenir snow-dome, newly shaken. The Sony Walkman had been invented the previous year, but I had an old Aiwa cassette player, like a toy piano, and a set of headphones.

> When the world is covered over
> and stars all shining bright
> we will make our escape
> into the night.

Then the bassline, just a single note with thirty-two drum-beats and fourteen seconds between each pluck of the string, suddenly shifts up one octave. At that moment, the terrestrial certainty of the song is entirely suspended. Suddenly you're up there, treading air, breathing heaven, before the bassline returns to its original plane and you're reunited with Planet Earth.

I once met Stephen Fellows, lead singer with the Comsat Angels. In a situation I'd probably fantasized about, he turned up at one of my readings. In Sheffield. 'You were in my favourite band,' I blurted out. 'We're still going,' he said. With a bunch of people from the bookshop we went out for something to eat afterwards, which also involved something to drink, and I think I blew it. If so, and if you ever get a chance to read this, Stephen, I'd just like to apologize, and to put it on record that 'Sleep No More' contains a few of the most euphoric and important musical minutes of my life. That song has been a metronome and a tuning fork and a compass bearing for me. I'd also like to apologize for another incident about two years later. Some time around August 1995, you might have a vague memory of being woken up by a ringing noise at about four in the morning. You didn't answer, but maybe you ran naked through the house trying to reach the phone before the answering machine cut in, and you heard the drunken voice of a man living on his own on the edge of Marsden Moor, discussing with himself the finer points of 'Sleep No More'. If so, I'm sorry. It was me.

Not being able to get a ticket for Arctic Monkeys' home-town gig for love nor money, I'm seeing them in Leeds, at the university. I taught here for a while, in the English Department, where the spectre of Geoffrey Hill still walked the corridors. Geoffrey Hill – the only living poet with a ghost. I don't believe Geoffrey is in the audience tonight, either in body or in spirit, though it would be hard to spot anyone in what seems to be a crowd of several thousand in a venue designed for considerably fewer. Most are students, which is a shame. I've got nothing against them as a body of people, but students at Leeds University tend to be from decent backgrounds where nutritious foodstuffs were in plentiful supply, which means they tend to be quite tall. So even at five eleven (six foot in certain footwear and after a few drinks) I'm going to struggle to see. Another problem with tonight's undergraduate audience is that many of them have never been to a gig before in their life, as evidenced by the way they're dressed. This isn't just about style; it's a question of practicality. A woman to my left is wearing a string of pearls. Her friend is wearing a ball gown. And anyone coming to a gig in a woolly jumper, a fleece or a toggled-up duffel coat, such as the guy about three rows in front of me, is either hoping to lose a lot of weight or is conducting a crude research project on self-combustion. Neither are tonight's audience particularly conversant with gig etiquette. One girl has brought a foldaway chair. One boy says 'Do you mind?' when he gets a bump from someone trying to pogo. On the plus side, it's good to see the lapel badge making a comeback, even it is a badge pinned to the lapel of a pre-distressed jacket from Burton or decorating the epaulette of a combat shirt in desert camouflage colours from some celebrity designer's latest range of post-Gulf, military-chic fashionwear. Not that I'm in any position to poke fun at the middle classes. About ten years ago I came with a friend to see The Fall at the same venue. There were only a couple of hundred people in the crowd, including a cat, but we still managed to work up a sweat at the front. Afterwards, as people waited for buses in the rain at the top of Woodhouse Lane or set off walking into darkest Leeds, we hopped over the wall into the staff car park. 'You could take that T-shirt off and wring it out,' my friend said to me. I said, 'Doesn't matter, I've got a fresh one in the glove compartment.'

Arctic Monkeys were catapulted to prominence by demos and downloads, or so the story goes, and without so much as a minute's airplay they were famous before anyone had heard of them. My friend Tony went to see them in Manchester a year ago and said they were going to be massive, and he wasn't wrong. He also said they'd brought a mob of their own followers with them – another bunch of people not familiar with gig etiquette – but not students this time. These were lads. A big gang of them. They were looking for trouble, and if they couldn't find it with the rest of the audience, they'd find it amongst themselves. Not nice, really. A disgrace, probably. But thankfully a useful number of them have breached campus security tonight and are giving it full whack at the front. It means that my definition of a good gig – more legs in the air than arms – is at least partially achieved. However, of all the things to rise above head height at a gig over the decades – hankies, flags, crowd-surfers, knickers, cigarette lighters and tape recorders – surely the least predictable was the camera-phone. It must be odd to be onstage, to lift your eyes away from your guitar for a moment and peer through your floppy fringe, only to be met by the gaze of a couple of hundred cyclopic Nokias and Samsungs and Sony Ericssons, all winking and flashing away.

The Low-down

♫

rewind rewind I'm no angel I've been unstable and unable and involved in bust-ups and dust-ups and I've had my fair share of flare-ups and tear-ups it starts with my brother a Gunner I swiped him a shirt did a runner got a slap from my mother but one thing leads to another your dad's boozing and losing the plot and pissing the lot down the toilet and so you go thieving and ducking and weaving and robbing till there's no way of stopping till it's just like shopping . . .

But here's the low-down this is Downview it isn't a showdown it's a slowdown there's a fountain there's a garden get a hairdo buy perfume get an en suite bathroom have a vacation get an education avoid temptation go to the gym keep trim learn decorating keep on medicating don't kick the block down they'll put you on lockdown loll around under the copper beech out of reach be ordinary learn the ancient art of falconry

rewind rewind I liked to do debit I went into finance and credit and plastic the scam was fantastic I did Visa and AmEx and keep getting flashbacks of fifty-pound cashbacks and did Es and did speed and at weekends went raving and generally misbehaving but don't get me going on bourbon or Stella I fight like an urban guerrilla I fight like a feller . . .

rewind rewind I worked as a dental nurse till I was a mental case
all that rinsing and spitting all the bad breath bored me to death
never want to see another incisor or a drop of saliva got offered a
job five grand cash in hand bringing coke over we're not talking
Pepsi or diet cola but where was the suitcase touched down and
got strip-searched fell at the final hurdle they put on the gloves
bend over the table I'll save you the trouble it's here in my girdle
I should have crotched it then I wouldn't have botched it . . .

I'm doing my time staying inside the yellow line keeping my
head down avoiding shakedown dodging a nervous breakdown
keeping myself to myself for the sake of my health some women
shack up but I'll smack up the bitch that rubs me up the wrong
way or gives me the eye inside I'm a block of ice I'm like stone
leave me alone if you've come here to talk about pain or the
strain of it all or the mess that you're in or the stress that you're
feeling or tell me how empty your marriage is just don't it's
embarrassing call the Samaritans . . .

But here's the low-down this is Downview it isn't a
showdown it's a slowdown there's a fountain there's a
garden get a hairdo buy perfume get an en suite bathroom
have a vacation get an education avoid temptation go to
the gym keep trim learn decorating keep on medicating
don't kick the block down they'll put you on lockdown
loll around under the copper beech out of reach be
ordinary learn the ancient art of falconry

♫

Sung by Claire in the film *Songbirds* (Century Films/
Channel 4, 2005).

On the Road 5

At a travel-writing panel discussion at the Adelaide Writers' Week I'm invited by the chairperson to elaborate on the essential difference between poets and novelists. I reply that in terms of travelling, the main distinction, as far as I can tell, is economy and business class. This is the third time I've been to Australia, and on each occasion the journey has ended in identical circumstances. At the end of the flight, I have peeled myself out of the back of the plane and stumbled towards the eye-stabbing daylight at the far end of the air-bridge. I am broken, stupefied, and on the verge of being overcome by my own fumes. In my slightly hallucinatory state I'm conscious of having two faces: my own, and imprinted upon it, the death mask of the man who slept next to me in row ninety-nine, a complete stranger whose cheek was glued to mine with body sweat for several unconscious hours, and not in any way the stranger I would have chosen when boarding the flight. After crawling towards the baggage-claim area and with focus gradually returning, I suddenly recognize the pristine outline of two or three UK authors – novelists – all looking as if they have been delivered by florists.

But enough moaning. The Aussies say they can tell when a flight of Poms has touched down, because even when the engines are cut the whining continues. I don't want to add to the high-pitched drone. And I'm being met in the arrivals hall by a friend of the festival who has evidently recognized me despite my facial disfigurement, and is waving a programme in my direction. I check in at the hotel and am handed over to another helper who suggests I might be hungry after such a long journey. I tell him that I think I probably am. 'Great,' he says, ''cause I could eat the crotch off a low-flying duck.' I take this to be a statement of his appetite rather than his tallness, although the image prompts me to reply that I could probably make do with a sandwich. Other Australian euphemisms are unpacked later in the day when a man delegated to chair one of my sessions says, 'If there aren't any questions from the audience, I'll throw you a Dorothy Dickser.'

'A what?'

'A Dorothy Dickser. You know, a free hit. But don't worry, I'll put a bit of spin on it. Don't just want to piss in your pocket, eh?'

I nod, agreeing that I wouldn't want him to do that either.

Adelaide is very bright and very, very hot. After breakfast – or maybe lunch, it's all a bit of a blur – I find the nearest pharmacy to purchase not just sunblock but several creams and emollients to combat a whole spectrum of living organisms from the fungal to the marsupial. I also try on at least a dozen pairs of sunglasses, every one of them strained or twisted in the same direction, it seems, given the way that a wide chevron of light opens to one side, like a car door left open, while on the other side the lens is squashed against my eyelash and cheek. I'm about to take this up with the store manager when an alternative – in fact statistically far more likely – explanation occurs to me, which is that my head is a parallelogram. Was it ever thus, or are Qantas to blame? Using my hand as a visor I grope my way back to the hotel and hit the pillow.

A fairly ordinary pillow, as it turns out, or at least a standard pillow. This much is implied by the 'Pillow Menu' propped on the bedside table. To the tired but wakeful traveller this offers a dozen options, from the Therapeutic Duel Support ('Anti-bacterial foam giving firm support with surface ridges reducing pressure points on the face') to the Firm Down-Filled ('80% grey goose down blended with 20% grey goose feather filling giving medium support') to what I imagine might be my pillow of choice, the V-Pillow, offering 'Comfortable neck and shoulder support for TV watchers and book readers'. My thoughts wander, to the room or vault somewhere beneath this colossal hotel, where the banks of pillows are housed. Some vast, cushioned warehouse, ballooning with clean white plumpness, where off-duty maids and receptionists bounce and tumble to their hearts' content. I also note, with some disappointment, that there is no pillow for the asymmetrical head.

The first formal engagement of the trip is breakfast on the lawn of Governor House with the governor of South Australia herself, Her Excellency Marjorie Jackson-Nelson, AC, CVO, MBE. Nicknamed the 'Lithgow Flash', Marjorie won two Olympic gold medals and seven Commonwealth gold medals, and broke the world sprint record on ten occasions. In a less mentionable moment she also dropped the baton in a fumbled exchange with

the perplexingly named Winsome Cripps on the last leg of the women's 4 × 100m relay with Australia way out in front. If life, as some theorists have speculated, is made up of a series of equal and opposite reactions, then perhaps Madge's baton blunder could be thought of as a counter-balance to Aussie speed-skater Steven Bradbury's bizarre achievement in the 2002 Winter Olympics, gliding over the finishing line from last place as the three men in front went base-over-apex in a wipeout on the final bend. Film footage of the incredulous Bradbury with arms aloft and a smile like a pumpkin slice has become one of Australia's favourite lengths of newsreel, and 'doing a Bradbury' has entered the national lexicon as a description of undeserved but much-celebrated success.

Doing a Bradbury might be the only way Team England can expect to find themselves amongst the medals at the Commonwealth Games, about to kick off in Melbourne. This isn't a criticism of their sporting ability, about which I know nothing, but a judgement based on their mode of transport from London Heathrow to Sydney, not in the front of the plane with the novelists and biographers, but rammed in the back with me. Quite how these finely honed athletes in their tracksuits and trainers are supposed to rescue their bodies from the contraction and contortion otherwise known as Flight QF200 is impossible to imagine. In the row behind me, I caught occasional glimpses of a large man I presumed to be a shot-putter or hammer-thrower, who slept in his narrow seat with both arms embedded deep within his ribcage, while the high-jumper next to him spent a day and a night with his knees up around his ears. I was also intrigued as to the diet of our lottery-funded hopefuls during the flight. Not macrobiotic meals vetted for supplements and steroids but, in the case of the young man sitting opposite, a swimmer perhaps, a family bag of beef-flavoured Hula Hoops and a packet of blackcurrant Chewits. Maybe he'd already heard the news that has saddened all of Australia, that swimmer Ian Thorpe, the man with dolphins instead of feet, has pulled out of the games.

The same person who recommends that I don't raise the baton-juggling episode with the governor also briefs me that the party in the garden is sometimes referred to as the Blue Rinse Breakfast. As I enter the grounds, I can certainly see a number of unnaturally coloured heads constellated around the tables on the lawns, some of them only marginally less vibrant than the exotic flora erupting from the beds and borders. But on table 27 I meet Thirza and Piers who are to become a surrogate aunt and uncle for the week. Piers is an Aussie, I guess, retired, I guess, and quietly content. Thirza is a book addict with an account at the local store. They own a house in the city and a 100-acre plot a couple of hours to the south where they feed kangaroos and garden in the nude. Thirza is originally from the Welsh valleys, and from the description of her new life in the southern hemisphere, I guess she isn't going back. At the Edinburgh Book Festival, a similar coming-together of writers and marquees, participating authors are offered use of the Yurt, a kind of upholstered igloo containing scatter cushions and whisky, which acts as a refuge from the rain and wind of the Scottish summer and as a hiding place from dissatisfied readers. Here in Adelaide, writers are afforded no such protection, and in the absence of any such bunker Thirza's coolbox becomes my oasis for the week. At 9.30 every morning she stakes out a prime position under the trees, and like a good nephew I am a prompt and frequent visitor. During one event, a ring-tailed possum trapezes between branches, and with intense, black eyes peers menacingly at the Booker-nominated prose stylist whose forthcoming bestseller disturbs his sleep.

Another lifeline is thrown to me by the writer Ben Rice, born in Devon but recently removed to Sydney with his Australian wife and child. Some years ago I gave his first book a good review, so as I see it he is obligated to my friendship, at least for this week, whether he wants it or likes it or not. In fact Ben strikes me as the sort of person who makes friends easily and naturally, without too much effort or fuss. Take, for example, Governor Marjorie, who invites Ben to a dinner party *inside* her residence and actually sits next to him. Furthermore, not only does she offer a frame-by-frame account of the baton incident, but after the meal leads him to a private drawing room to show him her medals (not a euphemism on this occasion). As the sketch continues, Ben is invited to accompany Mrs Jackson-Nelson on the piano as she sings a song about her sporting accomplishment, and this surreal musical interlude is only narrowly avoided when a member of staff interrupts with an important governmental message. As I pointed out in my review, Ben is a terrific storyteller.

Ben's other new friend in Adelaide, besides me, is the man in the Just Smokes cigarette kiosk off King William Street. Of Greek descent, we speculate, he has manic eyes and a big grin that widens to meet the conclusion of his witticisms and catchphrases. Accompanying Ben on his cigarette run, I notice a heavy, almost cosmetic darkness around the shopkeeper's eyes, which along with the thick black fringe and salamander pennant twisting on a tight leather necklace gives him the look of an Egyptian pharaoh. There could be worse afterlives, I guess, than doling out fags and funnies in sunny South Australia, 3,000 years after mummification and entombment. Come to that, isn't any life better than eternal death, or is that a naïve and annoyingly optimistic thought? Seriously, though, would any of us ever really drink from the Waters of Forgetfulness, to begin life again but with all memories of our previous life erased for ever? Offered a glass of that clear, obliterating liquid, wouldn't most of us push it to one side, preferring to remember and remain loyal to the person we are, no mater how painful or inconsequential our lives?

The owner of Just Smokes talks colourfully about some of the products on sale in the miniature shop, and is especially illuminating on the difference between hard-shell and soft-shell cigarette packets. Men prefer hard, he says, to protect the contents. Ben agrees. But women prefer the soft packets, which mould more willingly to their body shape, particularly when carried in the back pocket. Ben nods again and I nod with him. 'Yeeeeah,' says our man, stretching a single-syllable word across several seconds of time. For someone who doesn't smoke he has a good line on tobacco.

Society here isn't exactly classless, and it's quite possible that Adelaide has more inherited social divisions than other cities in Australia, the stratifications of the old country still alive and well in the minds of its huge expat population. But to me it feels like a country willing to speak its mind and not afraid to be judged by whatever comes out of its mouth. Not exactly Huddersfield in the sun, but I feel an affinity, or I forge one. The readings seem to go well, possibly because I feel so at home. More books have to be flown in from Sydney, which for a poet is not only unheard of but, according to some, inexplicable.

'Mate, you've done a Bradbury,' one man tells me.

After each session, members of the audience are invited to form a queue at a microphone stand and ask questions of the writers. I catch myself thinking about a child's birthday party I once went to in a suburb of Manchester, the high point of the celebration being a piñata, consisting of a coloured parcel full of toys and sweets suspended from a washing line slung across the back garden. With a variety of weapons including toy swords, light sabres, a garden rake and a pickaxe handle, most of the boys in the neighbourhood and some of the pluckier girls took it in turns to batter and club the piñata, beating the crap out of it until it spilled its guts.

At the book signing after my reading, the publicists or publisher's representatives pass along the queue, writing customers' names on little yellow Post-it notes and sticking them inside the books. When the book is presented to me I write the name on the Post-it on the title page and scrawl my signature underneath. The book is now not only signed but personalized, though why people should want a signed, personalized copy isn't always clear. Take Geoff, for example, in his canvas hat and Hawaiian shirt, who appears to have bought the entire Armitage boxed set, and informs me without a trace of embarrassment that he is going to 'bang the whole lot of 'em straight on eBay, mate'. Since I'm grateful for his custom I don't really want to contradict his business strategy, but surely there can only be a limited number of book buyers out there prepared to bid for a book of poems by Simon Armitage inscribed with the words 'To Geoff'. That said, my dad once bought a copy of Ned Sherrin's *Theatrical Anecdotes* inscribed with the words 'To C. Nixon Esq, with warm regards, Ned', and he seems perfectly pleased with it.

For the most part the Post-it system works very well. Misspellings are avoided this way, as are embarrassing misunderstandings, such as the time in Canterbury when I dedicated a book to someone I thought was called Monica.

'Who is Monica?' she asked, looking at the book in bewilderment.

'You're Monica,' I said.

'No,' she said. 'Your *moniker*.'

Then it was my turn to be bewildered. 'I'm not Monica,' I said.

The Post-it notes also help with what the publicity people call throughput, though most people still want to stop and chat for a couple of minutes, not usually about poetry but about Yorkshire. One woman says, 'Hello, I was conceived in Doncaster.' At the end of the session the table is covered with little yellow stickers, each one containing a reader's name. Doreen. Maggie. Kev. Kirsty. For a moment I have the absurd notion of keeping them all, putting them in a scrapbook. Evidence. Proof of something on days when the armies of Inferiority and Pointlessness smash down the fence and park their tanks on the lawn.

My final event of the week takes place on a boat, the *Popeye*, on the shallow, almost apologetic river at the bottom of the city. More like a boating lake in a council-owned park, its waters are greenish-brown in colour and slow to the point of giving no indication as to the direction of flow. Wherever the accumulated rainfall of this enormous landmass discharges into the sea, it is not here in Adelaide. We put-put upstream, I think, with unfeasibly big waterhens watching us from their nests in the reed beds and black swans tapping their red bills against the fibreglass hull, begging for scraps. There are about seventy or so of us, including the organizers, who circulate with trays of cheese cubes and bottles of red wine. Very quickly it gets very dark. To hear the readings the engines have to be cut, but then the poets can't see their poems because the lights are powered by the generator. Professionals to the last, we continue under the combined wattage of a pocket torch and a mobile phone. Even though there is more chance of dying of concussion than drowning in this river, I play it safe and read poems set on dry land and high mountains. More bravely and more appropriately, Judith Beveridge reads a sequence of fishing poems, including one about finding a child inside a shark. Then having done our stuff we're delivered safely ashore.

Water is not my element. It's got it in for me. Over the years, as a householder, I've suffered more forms of 'water ingress' than the insurance industry are prepared to accept, ranging from damp walls and wet rot to overflowing baths and burst pipes. The water main on the road outside once exploded, flooding the cellar in less than an hour. The water board didn't believe me. 'So what do you call that?' I asked the bloke in blue dungarees when he finally arrived in his Land Rover, three hours later. Staring down into five or six feet of clear, still water, he said, 'It's certainly a bit moist.'

1 Marjorie Armitage

2 Cry God for Harry, England and St George

3 Drummer Jack (*far right*)

4 & 5 Like father ... like son

6 Blackburn ahoy

7 Peter 'The Probation Officer' Armitage

8 Un-Reliant Robin

9 (*top*) Lest we forget

10 (*left*) Drinking licence

HOUSE OF COMMONS
LONDON SW1A 0AA

From Richard Wainwright M.P.

Dear Mr. Armitage,

    Congratulations! I see from the register of
electors that you are now eighteen. So you are now entitled
to vote.

    I am the Member of Parliament for your area, the Colne
Valley Constituency. I seek to represent every person, whatever
their political viewpoint. I take this opportunity of writing
to you, since, now you have the vote, you are probably keen to
find out what are the various political choices open to you.

    Please contact me if you would like any information of
any kind. Either write to me here at the House of Commons,
or contact my local office at 24 Westgate, Huddersfield.

    If I can ever be of any help in any other way, please do
not hesitate to contact me.

    With best wishes,

        Yours sincerely,

        Richard Wainwright, M.P.

hello simon heres the lyrics you asked for they are examples of a kind of stunted-prose, meant to leave holes for you to use. further information; pete becker and martyn bates meet and make attempts to speak through music, not in the cerebral way but merely by intuition — concerts feel strange to me; playing gigs thats what I'm talking about.... sometimes its a feeling that this is a good way of articulation; others, its a horrible sinking, ringing through you that you are mute....but then a moment each moment is to feel new things, but trying to decide how right they are!.. that the problem that always looms large.... *Martyn Bates*

11 Letters written

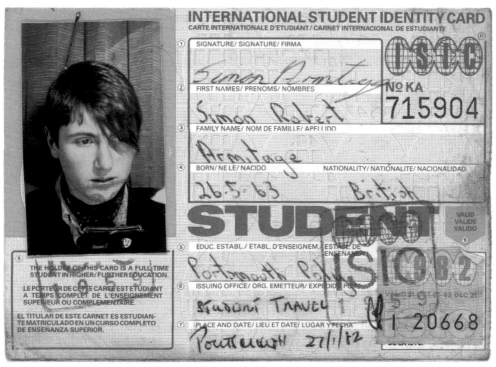

12 NUS card, New Romantic era

13 Surtsey: tarred and feathered

14 Surtsey: a rock and a hard place

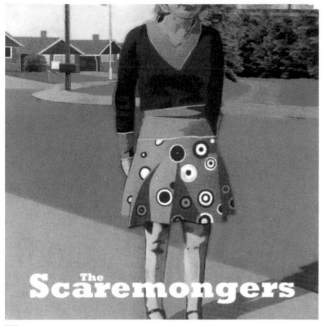

15 The Scaremongers: cover version

17 Scaremongering

18 A 'gig', Yorkshire Sculpture Park, 2007

On my first visit to Australia, to the Sydney Writers' Festival in 2002, a dozen or so authors were taken for a few days' R & R in the Hunter Valley, to get to know each other a little bit and to overcome the effects of jet lag before the readings. Our 'retreat' was Eaglereach Wilderness Resort, a hilltop encampment of luxury log cabins. We slept, ate, drank, talked and walked carefully around the hulking great kangaroos standing motionless in the middle of the dusty road. We were advised to keep our doors and windows closed to avoid intrusion by possums and bandicoots. There was only one phone on site, at the lodge, and one day a member of staff in his green polo shirt sauntered up to my cabin and told me my wife was on the other end of it. In New South Wales it was nine in the morning on a beautiful spring day, but in upstate Huddersfield it was a black, blustery night, slashing with rain, most of which was cascading through our roof. At the time we lived in one quarter of an old manor house that once belonged to a local magistrate by the name of George Armitage – no relation – who dispensed justice from the front porch. The architect who designed such a stately dwelling in the early eighteenth century wasn't stupid, and neither were the businessmen who renovated it in the 1970s and divided it into four. Three sides of the house were dressed with ashlar stone and surrounded by formal lawns, but our bit – the old serving quarters, presumably – was constructed of less elegant material and faced north. And whereas the front of the house enjoyed views, sunlight and privacy, the back of the house received the brunt of the wind, the noise of the traffic, and vast quantities of rain. Not just the rain as it fell from heaven, but the rain from the whole of the building as it drained from the tiled roofs and was channelled in our direction via a valley gutter. During downpours, that asphalted valley was like a torrent, with many gallons of water per second surging over our heads towards a single fall pipe above the front door, usually blocked with dead leaves or dead birds. On this particular morning, though – or this evening, I should say – the fall pipe is not an issue, because most of the river of water has found an alternative route. At the end of the line on the other side of the world, Speedy Sue says, 'So what are you going to do about it?' It's fair enough. She has a point to make and she makes it well. She's in thundery West Yorkshire single-handedly holding back the elements, while I'm in a sun-kissed wine-growing region at the opposite side of the planet.

'I am *working*,' I say, immediately wishing I hadn't.

In the background I can hear the Tudge laughing and giggling and splashing about in the puddles on the carpet.

'That my bucket, that my bucket,' she says.

'No, leave it there. Leave it . . .'

'Oh, that wet. My bucket done wet.'

The phone call continues, to a soundtrack of such authentic watery noises that I start to think Speedy Sue might be exaggerating the crisis by playing a BBC sound effects tape, just to make me feel worse. Eventually, there's only one thing left to say, and finally, inevitably, I say it.

'Why don't you call Dad?'

'I already did.'

'Is he coming?'

'He's already here.'

'Put him on the phone.'

'I can't.'

'Why not?'

'He's on the roof.'

And so he is. With his mate Gordon. They've put a dustbin by the back door and climbed above the kitchen. They've crawled across the stone apex and shinned up to the next level, on to the leaded surface above the study, then would have had to edge over the moss-covered slates twenty-five feet above the yard to drop down into the valley gutter. In the driving wind and hammering rain, now they're manhandling large, heavy sheets of tarpaulin and trying to divert the oncoming surge with their clothes and their limbs. Gordon, who suffers from vertigo, and my dad, who suffers from seasickness, are up in the rigging, trying to steady the ship. Now I can hear another soundtrack, which includes the uttering of unrepeatable northern oaths, and the sound of large, heavy feet on a thin roof. Then the line goes dead. I wait by the phone for a while but it doesn't ring. I feel guilty and useless. But there's absolutely nothing I can do, and back at the cabin the Californian novelist I'm sharing with is floating in the outdoor jacuzzi and has opened a rather good chilled Sémillon Chardonnay. And I've just slipped down into the bubbles when I remember that the part of the house which now sounds to be partially submerged – the long corridor beneath the long valley gutter – is where I keep my records.

Maybe that house was cursed. In an oddly antithetical crisis, a year or two later I was driving home with the

Tudge in the back of the car only to find a crowd of people outside the front gate and a plume of smoke rising from somewhere over the wall.

'Don't go in there,' one bloke shouts.

'It's my house,' I shout back.

In the yard, an old man is lying face down on the cobbles while the front end of his Reliant Robin is blazing away against the house. Apparently these infamous three-wheelers, otherwise known as plastic pigs, do have a tendency to burst into flames every now and again. And when the cabin of this particular vehicle had started filling with smoke, its eighty-one-year-old driver had decided the best course of action would be to steer it into our front garden, a difficult enough manoeuvre even in a car which is not on fire but one that he had executed with great aplomb. Then he'd bailed out, abandoning the fireball of his vehicle as it trundled towards the wooden garage door.

'Smelly red smoke, Daddy,' says the Tudge. I sweep her up, charge round the front of the house and deposit her with the neighbours – the neighbours who are blissfully unaware that the rear portion of their residence is ablaze. On returning, the old man has been dragged to safety by one of the onlookers. Why isn't the valley gutter overflowing when you need it? I'm thinking. And where's the bastard fire brigade? I scream at a woman with a shopping bag who has nothing better to do on a Saturday afternoon than watch my house burn to the ground.

'I've called them, they're on their way,' she says.

They arrive in a matter of minutes, but minutes take a long time when smoke is beginning to appear in your bedroom window, and desperate to do something, anything, I have sprinted across the yard, opened the front door and climbed the stairs.

The subject of what to rescue from your burning house is often broached in the lifestyle pages of the Sunday papers. The answer, once all kith and kin are accounted for, is very often the cat. We don't have a cat. Even in a blind panic, among the fumes, I'm pretty sure about that, though I seem to be less certain of other facts. Where do we keep the photograph albums? Is it here by the bulk-head, or in the chest of drawers in the spare room? Maybe I should take Speedy Sue's wedding dress. But would that be beautiful, or would it be melodramatic, sycophantic even? Anyway, is it hanging in the wardrobe shrouded in plastic or is it folded in a suitcase under the bed? I walk into my office – the room nearest the fire. The laptop and floppy disks are sitting on the desk, but if I took those items and not the photographs or the wedding dress, where would that leave me? In the doghouse, probably. Now I'm in the Tudge's bedroom. I could grab an armful of soft toys, but they'd almost certainly be the wrong ones, only reminding her that her favourite dolls and furry friends have perished in the flames. I close all the upstairs doors. Now I'm in the dark, windowless corridor below the valley gutter, with just enough natural light to notice the row of albums stacked against the wall. My record collection. My own bodyweight in vinyl. Too much even to lift, let alone carry. Fuck it, I think. I'd rather have nothing than just one or two. Let it merge and melt. I make a last, mad tour of the house, and emerge with just two items. The first is the buildings and contents insurance policy. A very good choice. My second selection is inexplicable, except perhaps as a counterbalance to the icy-cold logic and clinical rationale of the insurance policy. It is a cactus.

Outside, a fire engine is in the yard and men in hard yellow hats are pumping water on to the remains of the car and the roof of the house. A fireman with an axe asks me if I keep anything of a flammable nature in the garage. No, I tell him. He smashes the wooden coal hatch, climbs in through the hole, and immediately climbs back out carrying a can of petrol. Apart from that, I say. Then there's nothing else to do apart from sit back and watch. And phone Dad, of course, because it's a crisis. An ex-fireman, he turns up a little while later and casts his eye over the smouldering, steaming mess.

'What's the damage?' I ask him.

'It's nowt,' he says.

Then he lights his pipe.

The house withstands the flames. The old man lives. Of his car, all that exists to remind us of its former status as a motor vehicle is the frame of the seat. Everything else is gloop and dust.

'Who was that on the phone?' my dad asks.

'The garage. They're coming round with a tow-truck,' I say.

'Ring 'em back. Tell 'em they'd be better off with a dustpan and brush.'

Even though I couldn't possibly have orchestrated it, especially not from 17,000 miles away, I wonder sometimes if the incident which required my dad to take to the roof in a thunderstorm was actually some kind of revenge. My parents live in an end terrace on the edge of the moor. For as long as I've been their son they've lived in that house, and they don't look like moving. Why should they? It's comfortable, quiet, has a large front window that overlooks the whole of the village, and is within walking distance of my dad's usual watering holes. The house hasn't changed that much since I moved out. Three-piece suites have come and gone; the wooden sash windows and wooden front door have been replaced by glossy, low-maintenance uPVC; walls have been repapered or coloured with whiter shades of pale. But the telly still squats in the far corner, staring back, and the piano is still parked in the alcove of the extension, and the extension is still referred to as 'the extension' twenty-five years after it was built. Despite children and grandchildren, the row of pot animals along the front of the bookshelf maintains pretty much the same formation, although the donkey now wears a sticking plaster on his leg, and sunlight occasionally exposes a fracture or a trace of superglue on the limbs and antlers of other members of the menagerie. The same foldaway table, located behind the armchair, still comes into play, either on social occasions when a plate of digestives or a tray of sweetcake is introduced into the proceedings, or when the Tudge sits down for a TV teatime, just as I did, and my sister before me. Her seat is the 'pouf', a sort of upholstered chest, like a little throne with a lift-up lid. If a new settee arrives, the pouf gets a makeover in matching fabric, and the same wooden frame must have worn at least a dozen colours by now. I haven't looked inside the pouf for several years but imagine it still contains my mother's sewing kit and the box of buttons handed down over time, buttons fallen or snipped from the cardigans and uniforms of long-dead ancestors. And my dad's ashtray still occupies its position on the carpet next to the waste-paper bin. Banned from smoking in the house during a crackdown in the early nineties, he generally obliges by smoking in the garden, fumigating the patio with St Bruno ready-rubbed or exhaling from the veranda of his makeshift shed and watching the knots and curls of white smoke go twisting off along the Colne Valley. On the occasions when he does contravene the rule of law by lighting his pipe in the living room, he kneels on the hearth rug in front of the coal-effect fire and evacuates his smoke by blowing it up the chimney. I've never worked out if this is a gesture of consideration or one of selfishness, i.e. is it undertaken as a courtesy to my mum and a concession to her feelings about smoke, or is it simply to avoid detection and escape a bollocking?

The other thing that hasn't changed is the cellar. To enter my parents' home by the front door is to find yourself in a narrow corridor, a kind of airlock between the outer world and the inner house, always referred to as 't'passage'. T'passage is home to 't'cubby 'ole', a dumping ground for erroneous shoes and rogue footwear, set into the wall. The entrance to the kitchen is cunningly concealed by a sliding door, an unintentional *trompe l'œil* which appears to be part of a dividing wall. So to the unannounced guest or unwelcome intruder, once trapped inside t'passage with no light to steer by other than the glow of the boiler, the only feasible exit would appear to be the door directly ahead. Tripped by a loose welly or stray slipper, the unfortunate visitor now accelerates towards that door, which, being unlocked and all too ready to swing open, offers no useful resistance. Immediately beyond it begins a dark, floorless void, a stone stairway without landing or handrail. So neither foot nor hand finds anything other than air. The laces of walking boots on a shelf overhead might pass across the face like fake cobwebs on the ghost train at Blackpool, but other than that, there's nothing to break the unstoppable momentum of a falling body in its descent to the dungeon. Even screaming is futile, as the polystyrene tiles on the wall and ceiling of t'passage (still bearing the prodded impression of my cricket bat handle) absorb all vocal expressions of terror.

Modern houses tend not to have cellars. It makes sense. Cellars are smelly places. Many cellars in West Yorkshire have small streams running through them. Toads live there. Put metal in a cellar and it rusts. Put wood in a cellar and it goes mouldy. Put food in a cellar and it rots. Put a bucket of water in a cellar and the next day a family of dead mice will be floating in it. Cellars are often described by estate agents as 'below-floors storage areas' or even 'wine vaults' if the ceiling is remotely curved. But cellars are cellars, home to pests, fungus and strange noises in the middle of the night. Some time during the eighties, my dad decided to paint our cellar, and he decided to paint it blue. Or maybe green – in the dimly lit netherworld beneath the house it's never been easy to tell. It was a decision based on availability, however, rather than taste. I don't know who supplied the paint, but let's say it didn't come with a receipt. Neither did it come with any kind of guarantee of behaving like paint. To this day the walls of the cellar are still an unspecific shade of greenish-blue, or bluish-green, and to this day the paint has not dried. Rest your hand against the surface and a dollop of something moist and creamy – like cold, wet eyeshadow – comes away on the skin. Lean your backside or shoulder against it and your clothes are ruined. All members of the Armitage family know to descend into the cellar with their arms flat to their sides and to steer a middle line. Perhaps to help us hold our course, or perhaps because he'd obtained a further supply of knock-off emulsion, my dad took a paintbrush to the outer edges of the steps and painted them white. It looked like a no-parking zone. The white paint didn't dry either, so if you were to stray from the straight and narrow, as well as the aquamarine elbow patches and turquoise cuffs you could find yourself leaving tacky white footprints along t'passage and down the street. In fact most things in that cellar appeared to exist in a semi-fluid state, either through dampness in the winter or through condensation at the height of the summer, when the very stone seemed to sweat. Everything, that is, apart from a large iron pan with a copper-coloured lid and a long, Bakelite handle. Like every cellar I ever entered as a child, ours contained a large stone table, 't'slab'. And on that slab sat the cornerstone of every meal: the chip pan. A sticky cauldron of solidified lard, it took at least half an hour for the fat to melt over a gas ring. Once molten and smoking hot, an apparently unlimited quantity of chipped potatoes could be tipped into it and were ready to be scoffed in a matter of minutes. Then after each meal, with the boiling-hot fat slopping around inside it, and now resembling something more like a medieval device for repelling raiders than a cooking utensil, the chip pan was returned downstairs to its charred and fat-stained landing pad on the stone slab. Where it lived. And while everything else in the cellar continued its slow evolution towards liquefaction and structural meltdown, the contents of the chip pan hardened into a dense block.

Milk was sometimes kept on the slab, because the stone stayed cool. We did have a fridge, but unlike anything I've ever heard of before or since it was a gas-powered fridge, with a little exhaust pipe on top. When the pilot light went out, which it did with great regularity, a Corgi-registered plumber was required to perform the reignition ceremony, though this didn't stop my dad fiddling around behind it with a plastic torch and a box of Swan Vestas. I guess the fridge was cheap, or at least cheaper than its electric counterpart, because although we were not against advances in technology we preferred them if they arrived with some kind of discount. When a telephone was eventually installed, we signed up for something called a 'party line'. By sharing the service with another user – a neighbour – it meant we saved a few quid every quarter. It also meant that while I was talking to my girlfriend, I could be interrupted at any moment by the farmer at the top of the road asking if I'd get off the line for a few minutes while he negotiated the price of pigswill or talked to the slaughter-man about a dead cow in his field.

The milkman brought the milk. The fish man brought the fish. The pop man brought the pop. The egg man brought the eggs and they were kept on the slab as well. So were cans of soup and beans. But there wasn't just one room in the cellar, there were two, and if those rooms could be categorized as 'his and hers' (and thinking of my parents as pretty traditional when it came to the gender divide) then the first room, with the slab and the chip pan and the tinned supplies, belonged to my mum, and the second room, furthest from the light and deepest below ground, belonged to my dad. Notionally a storeroom, it was in fact a dumping ground for obsolete machinery and useless goods. It was also a shrine to Dad's haphazard approach to DIY. Other men in the area, 'knacklers' by nature, seemed to have dedicated their entire lives to making something out of nothing. They had constructed pigeon lofts from old pallets. They had made workbenches from broken chairs. With nothing more than a trowel and a bucket, the father of a friend of mine had excavated an entire room from the mud beneath his kitchen floorboards. The following summer he had gone on to install central heating and a bar, and was brewing his own stout by the barrelful. Tools were stored on template-board, where the neatly drawn outline of a hacksaw or a drill described the tool's absence and encouraged its return. He'd even converted an old doll's house into a portable storage unit, so when the façade of the model Georgian mansion swung open it offered dozens of pull-out plastic trays containing nuts, bolts and nails, all of them sorted and sized. Men such as my friend's dad made order out of chaos. My dad seemed to approach DIY if not from an opposite direction then at least from a more oblique angle, covering up chaos with a veneer of order, beneath which, and not very far from the surface, chaos was ready to re-emerge. True, he'd fitted shelves to one wall of the storeroom, and the shelves themselves were lengths of old skirting board put to good use. But rather than fixing them with brackets, he'd hung them on bits of old electrical flex suspended from huge nails driven into the mortar with a lump-hammer. An old wardrobe, minus some component necessary to its erectness, was propped in the corner like a tired old boxer at the end of a particularly savage round. I've never understood the older generation's fascination with oilcloth, or the need to own a length of it 'just in case'. But sure enough a thick and heavy roll of the stuff lay slumped across the floor where it had fallen several years before, like a dead body left to rot. And the sense of that room as some kind of funereal underworld was only increased by the presence of several ex-army uniforms from the Crimean War rammed in a metal chest under an old table. The macabre pile of bayoneted jackets and bloodstained trousers had turned up in an old foundry, and was en route to a military museum or theatrical outfitter's. But for as long as they lay in the back cellar of my parents' house, they lent a chilling and ghostly atmosphere to a room that was spooky enough in the first place. Even in the middle of the day, with the light on, it wasn't somewhere I liked to venture. Nevertheless, about once a month, I was invited to slither head first into the horrible darkness. The guillotine-style metal hatch at the back of the house would be drawn upwards, a nod of encouragement would come my way, and down the coal chute and into the darkness I would slide.

I'm pretty certain I was born in a period of history when key-cutting was a well-established practice and when the key fob was a readily available and relatively cheap item of merchandise. But memory tells me that we only owned one key to the house and that this was kept in my mother's purse. My mum being a very careful person, it meant that the key was never lost. It also meant that the key often remained in the cupboard where she kept the purse, when it should have been with us, on the pavement, on the other side of the latched door, being put to the purpose for which it was designed. This little sketch often took place at ten or eleven at night, having arrived back from a family outing or one of my dad's shows. He'd probably be wearing his dinner jacket and dicky bow. Mum would have had her hair done and she'd be wearing a flowery dress. Me and my sister would be togged out in our Sunday best. Despite the fact that only one key existed and we all knew exactly where it was, we'd all put on a little show of checking our pockets and looking under plant pots. Then came the inevitable journey to the back of the house, and the grating and scraping of metal on metal as the coal hatch was raised. The impenetrable darkness stared back at us. Dad was too big. Mum shouldn't – not with the dress and the hair. And my sister, being older and less biddable, simply pulled rank and refused.

Down I went. There was no coal – we had a gas fire. And a gas fridge. But there were sacks of spanners, like bones. And the ghosts of dead soldiers. And the lurching wardrobe. And the murdered oilcloth. With my hands out in front of me, checking for child-killers and supernatural apparitions, I'd grope my way out of the back cellar, into the front cellar, then on past t'slab (now a sacrificial altar) towards the stairs. Heading upwards it was impossible not to have at least one encounter with slimy blue paint, to experience the clammy ectoplasm between the fingers, or to feel against the face the tentacles of bootlaces dangling from the shelf overhead. At the age of eight I wasn't familiar with the myth of Orpheus but I knew instinctively not to look back. At the head of the stairs was a light switch. Then t'passage. Then the door. I'd flick the latch and swing it open. They'd be waiting on the step, vaguely grateful but keen to push past me and get warm. Mum would say it was time for bed. If he'd had a few drinks and was still buzzing, Dad would say, 'Come on, let's have something to eat. Simon, go and get the chip pan.'

Man Versus Machine

On long trips, relieve the boredom by pitting your wits against your iPod. Wire the iPod through the car stereo, set it to Shuffle Songs, and turn it face down on the passenger seat. The game then is to guess the name of the song, the album it's from and the group or artist before the song ends. A point to yourself for every correct answer, a point to the iPod for every wrong answer, and there's a bonus point for saying the song title before it's actually announced in the lyrics. It's harder than you think, and even more difficult if you've downloaded Volumes 1 and 2 of *The Independent's Guide to British Bird Song*. On a recent return trip to Taunton, it was neck and neck all the way up the M6. Then coming off Saddleworth Moor with the score at a nerve-jangling 97 to Armitage and 98 to the little white box, I mistook a lapwing for a ring ouzel, and crossed the finish line at the bottom of the drive a beaten man.

On the Road 6

Never make the mistake of asking Australians if they 'pop over to New Zealand very often'. 'No,' they'll tell you. 'Do you pop over to Moscow?' Tonight I understand. It's a long way, and even longer if you're at the back of the plane. Again. When I get there, the hotel isn't finished. The carpet is sheeted in plastic and the lift is lined with cardboard. But inside the room two shapes emerge from the darkness – Speedy Sue (of Sue and the Speedy Bears fame) and the Tudge. Eighteen and a half thousand miles from home, it's a kind of homecoming.

Wellington is a kind of mini-city. It has tall buildings and cappuccinos, it has motorways and a university, it has vagrants and botanical gardens, but all pretty much within walking distance and all gathered around the bay, like furniture around a TV. The more interesting areas, perversely enough, are the suburbs, consisting of colourful wooden houses dotted around the hills and foot-slopes. Crazy, zigzagging steps climb the impossibly steep slopes between them, and some have their own hand-cranked cable cars operating between garden and beach. The very biggest houses at the top of each summit all belong to Peter Jackson, according to the taxi drivers. New Zealand is in the grip of movie fever, the entire landscape having been rebranded as a film set almost overnight. In a country where sheep are famously said to outnumber humans by ten to one, the next most numerous creature is now the film extra. 'I was an orc,' says the guide on a seal-watching tour. His cousin was an elf. In the tourist information offices, along with maps and timetables, the *Lord of the Rings Location Guidebook* is on prominent display and in plentiful supply. Not that this extraordinary country needs to be overlaid or underwritten by fiction – the actual landscape is sufficiently unreal in its own right. On one particular day, we swim in the sea, sunbathe on the beach, then drive through pampas grass and subtropical forest, then power-boat through a canyon carved by melt-water, then land in a helicopter on the top of a glacier. It's an oddly compacted geography of landscapes and climates, and to the 'westernized' mindset it comes as something of a surprise. We don't expect clean air and pure water to be found in such close proximity to cashpoint machines and cafe culture. Or don't deserve them, maybe.

There's a function at the Governor General's residence, or the Governor General and Commander-in-Chief in and over New Zealand, to give Dame Silvia Cartwright her full title. Government House is situated at the top of a long, curling driveway not far from the cricket ground. Queen Elizabeth II stares from one wall, and from the opposite wall Queen Victoria stares back. Signed photographs of the royal family are arranged on the piano. The reception is for everyone connected with the International Festival, not only writers but sword-swallowers, fire-eaters, meerkat impersonators, penis-puppeteers, etc. The Tudge says, 'I think I'm going to fall to the floor,' and we take her outside to play football on the lawn with a pine cone.

On a midweek afternoon, a handful of visiting writers take the opportunity of a guided walk around the Karori Wildlife Sanctuary on the outskirts of the capital. In the minibus, our guide – an expert on native species – begins by explaining that despite the best efforts of the British to treat it as a flat, blank canvas, Wellington is a city of hills. Of all the crimes my home country can rightly be accused of, I didn't expect to have to add altitude-ism to the list. Surely the evil colonizers knew a contour when they came across one? All the same, I oblige with a suitably culpable nod of the head when he glances in my direction. The reserve is a safe haven, bordered by a heavy-duty prison-style fence extending several metres into the air and a good few into the ground, which throws its protective arms around many a rare plant and creature. As well as keeping kiwi and other endangered species in, the fence keeps out unwanted stoats and rats. Again, the weasels at the back of the minibus are to blame, predatory pests being two of Britain's more successful exports. So again I nod, in a weaselly kind of way, and put my sunglasses on.

The area we are about to walk in is either a little patch of Eden before the Fall or an allotment of eco-nationalism, depending on how right-on or contrary you happen to be feeling. Teri from Chicago says, 'So it's like some kinda Jurassic Park, right?' a comment which goes unnoticed by our guide who is explaining the first principles of Darwinism to Armand Leroi, reader in Evolutionary Developmental Biology at Imperial College. I've left my binoculars in the hotel, which is truly disappointing, because the ornithology is extraordinary, though not as extraordinary as our ears would have us believe. At the foot of Birdsong Gulley we marvel at the sudden and spontaneous squawking and fluting of several rare species, unaware that the Tudge has run on ahead, triggering the birdsong soundtrack now being broadcast from speakers hidden in the trees. However, there's nothing synthetic about the fantails, tui, tomtits and bellbirds we see as we make our way around the trail. There's even kaka – a weird, lumbering bush parrot with a pink-red underside – wobbling around in a branch just over our heads. The American poet Robert Hass very sweetly offers me a go with his bins, but there's something not right about fiddling with the focus on another man's field glasses, especially when they're still connected to his neck by the strap.

Of all New Zealand's towns and cities, the small and tidy tourist centre of Queenstown contains the highest number of refugees from Middle Earth. Most of its inhabitants claim to have popped up in at least one of the *Lord of the Rings* films with either a warty head or pointy ears, though happily they seem to have dropped their Norfolk/ Somerset accents and no longer speak in riddles. Next to his photo ID, our taxi driver proudly points to a kids' trading card that displays some savage-looking beast with a latex face and big plastic teeth. 'That's me,' he says. Only able to see the back of his head as he drives, the Tudge hides under her mother's arm, just in case he turns around.

From Queenstown we strike out into staggering countryside, none more staggering than the road between Te Anau and Milford Sound. I've never read any of those crap-sounding books called things like *100 Trips to Make*

Before You Croak, and probably won't bother if this particular stretch of the planet doesn't figure in the index. Each bend in the road offers a scene more outrageously spectacular or bewildering than the last, including the sudden epiphany of the Eglinton Valley, its lazy, pebbly river moseying through a flood plain of sashaying yellow grass, overlooked by looming, steaming mountains. Obviously you couldn't live here, which is why hardly anyone does. I glance at an isolated farmhouse in the middle distance, the only sign of civilization in the visible world, and know with absolute certainty that after three or four weeks in a place like this I would have shot my dog and would be hanging from the nearest tree. Elsewhere, mile-high walls of glistening black rocks with razor-sharp ridges bear down on mirror-lakes and white-water rivers, or pioneering wooden bridges span valleys of thick, jungle-looking woodland, or slabs of mountains stand as impenetrable obstacles until the miraculous and implausible appearance of some roughly driven tunnel or hand-carved road. Behind the avuncular-looking, snow-dusted, white-haired summits, dark-pointed peaks wait in line, like witches queuing up to piss in the baby's cradle. Languid, red-legged Australasian harriers fall on succulent rodents in the fields, or parachute towards the abundance of roadkill, possum and the like lying squashed and smeared on the metalled surface. The menu of pavement pizza includes the harriers themselves, splattered while dining, killed by the very means that offered them their meal.

I can't understand how these roads were built. I have difficulty in understanding it as a human accomplishment.

Wouldn't it take a million years to lay just a hundred miles of tarmac through such unyielding country? Where did the gravel come from? The display board at Milford Sound tells us that the first road was laid by three men with pickaxes and wheelbarrows. Surely this is astronomical bullshit. Surely only the Romans, or NATO, or aliens, could have forged a traversable passageway across this untraversable terrain. Of course, all this is as nothing to the Tudge, sprawled across the back seat, eyes glued to a portable DVD, ears plugged in to my iPod. Over the last week of travelling, and possibly as a reaction to boredom, she has become aware, for the first time in her life, of the pleasures of irony. For example, watching a film while listening to a separate soundtrack. Or, more specifically, watching the camcorder version of my dad's latest panto, *Mutiny on the Bounty*, performed by the Yorkshire Avalanche Dodgers, while listening to 'Nocturn' by Kate Bush, an orgasmic song about skinny-dipping at dusk on Midsummer Eve and resurfacing at dawn, as far as I can tell. So with the holiday of a lifetime sliding past the car window, thirty or so grass-skirted northerners – the sons of Tetley – bounce their beer bellies and flex their tattoos to the strains of the rejuvenated Ms Bush bringing herself to vocal and lyrical climax.

On the Road 7

New Zealand International Arts Festival, March 2006. At the book signing:

Woman: Can you sign this, please?
Me: Is it for you?
Woman: It's for my feller.
Me: What's his name?
Woman: Spaz.
Me: Spaz? As in . . . spaz?
Woman: Yes.
Me: Are you sure?
Woman: Yes. He's from Burnley.

On the Road 8

New Zealand International Arts Festival, March 2006. At the book signing, the next day:

> Woman: Hello again.
> Me: Hello.
> Woman: This is Spaz.
> Me: Hello, Spaz.
> Spaz: Can I ask you a question about writing?
> Me: Sure.
> Spaz: When you told people in Huddersfield you were a poet, didn't you get your head kicked in?

Melek's Lullaby

♫

How many miles to the nearest town?
Twenty miles and ten.
Can I get there with an English pound?
Yes and back again.
My son and my daughter, my sun and my moon,
it won't be for ever,
it won't be soon.

How many miles to my daughter's cot?
Twenty miles and ten.
Can I get there with a knife and fork?
Yes, and back again.
My son and my daughter, my sun and my moon,
it won't be for ever,
it won't be soon.

How many miles to my little boy's thumb?
Twenty miles and ten.
Can I get there with a plastic comb?
Yes and back again.
My-son and my daughter, my sun and my moon,
it won't be for ever,
it won't be soon.

Gig

How many miles to my father's fist?
Twenty miles and ten.
Will he still raise his bamboo stick?
No, girl, never again.
My son and my daughter, my sun and my moon,
it won't be for ever,
it won't be soon.

How many years till they set me free?
Twenty miles and ten.
Do my boy and my girl remember me
every now and then?
My sun and my moon, my daughter and son,
do you hear me singing,
do you know who I am?

♫

Sung by Melek in the film *Songbirds* (Century Films/ Channel 4, 2005).

Morrissey
King George's Hall, Blackburn
11 May 2006

What is Blackburn?

I don't mean that disparagingly – how can I? I'm from Huddersfield. I'm just genuinely curious. Is it like Bolton, or is it Oswaldtwistle? Is it the ink-blot version of Halifax on the opposite side of the Pennines? Or is it Barnsley? Is it Keighley? In the late seventies, rather than going on proper holidays to the coast or even abroad, my father hired a sixty-foot narrowboat and we cruised the English water-ways. It sounds idyllic, but there was a catch. Several in fact. The barge, the *Lady Rhodes*, was actually owned by Greater Manchester Probation Service, and was only available when not providing pleasure cruises to gangloads of

Mancunian car thieves and smack addicts. (Because the road to recovery is not the pavement but the towpath.) So the vessel carried the scars of its employment, usually in the form of hand-carved graffiti or the occasional burnt teaspoon, and the smell of Old Holborn never quite left the air. Added to which, the waters we travelled were not the clear-running brooks of the fields and meadows or the reed-lined watercourses of the Norfolk Broads but the stagnant canal that connected several depressed Lancashire cotton towns before discharging into Liverpool Docks. In Blackburn, moored overnight near the lock-keeper's cottage, we were pelted with dog shit by several of the local youth. I don't think they meant any lasting harm; there was probably nothing else to do on a Friday night in central Lancashire other than stand on the road bridge and lob animal excrement at Yorkshire people. Also, at that time, the canals of post-industrial northern Britain were considered to be little more than unofficial soil pipes; if we were weird enough to spend our summer holidays on an open sewer, a bit more shit wasn't going to harm. Hilariously, we sometimes dangled a fishing rod over the side, and on one lunatic occasion actually put on our swimming trunks and jumped in. In a photograph from one of those holidays I'm a skeletal sixteen-year-old sporting a home-made haircut. I'm perched at the front of the vessel with a rope in my hand, about to perform some complicated nautical manoeuvre. In what looks like a fairly pathetic attempt to let other canal users know that I wasn't just some simple-minded barge-hand but a cool and truculent teenager, I'm wearing a Jam T-shirt. Even more pathetically, the writing on the shirt is slightly smudged from where I'd run a steam iron across it. I wanted to spit in the face of authority, obviously, but I wasn't going to do it in a creased shirt.

Blackburn bought the Premiership title in 1994/95, pipping United by one point, and Condoleezza Rice came here recently, and was photographed at Ewood Park holding a no. 10 Rovers shirt with her surname on it. Behind her, the then Foreign Secretary and MP for Blackburn grinned and dribbled.

'So are you ashamed of Jack Straw?' Morrissey asks the audience.

No clear answer one way or another.

'Well, you should be.'

I once gave a poetry reading in Blackburn in a nightclub, but don't recall if it was at the near-legendary Jazzy Kex just off Barbara Castle Way, or Jumpin' Jaks, described by one contributor to the *Knowhere Guide* as 'a pile of shite' (clearly a preoccupation in Blackburn). I remember very little about it apart from using the tombola machine as a lectern.

'All you Jimmy Clitheroes out there,' says Mozzer.

Boating through Blackburn one summer, I made the mistake of hooking a carrier bag out of the water with the bargepole. The dense and colourful-looking contents turned out to be the sodden fur of several drowned kittens.

'In Halifax the other night I felt very . . . blessed. Well, I'm sorry but I did. And I feel it again tonight. Thank you, Blackburn.'

A cheer, which is actually a roar.

Then, 'Disgusting to hear about animal rights activists

getting forty years.' (He doesn't give the full details of the offence in which the remains of an old lady were snatched from a grave and dumped in a nearby wood.) 'Just for caring about animals.'

Muted response. Then somebody shouts something, possibly about a bacon sandwich.

Morrissey: 'Oh, aren't I allowed to say anything?'

Various replies – none meaningful.

'So do you want me to go?'

'NOOOOOOOOOOOOOOOOOOOOOOOOOOO.'

The chorused answer doesn't surprise me, and probably doesn't surprise Morrissey either, because it's quite possible that many of the people in King George's Hall tonight were also in the crowd at Preston Guild Hall in 1986. On that occasion, the Smiths are only two minutes into their first song, 'The Queen is Dead', when a missile rumoured to be a ten-pence piece hits him on the head and sends him spinning to the ground. Clutching his face, he marches from the stage and the band trudge off after him. Then the house lights come up and a very nervous voice hiding behind the PA system explains that Morrissey has been injured and the show is over. For some unlucky people, those two minutes of strobing lights, swirling guitar and stampeding drums were as much of the Smiths as they would ever see. A furiously disappointed crowd spilled out on to the streets of Preston that night, apparently, with their flowers still in cellophane. To this day, nobody really knows if Morrissey's injury was actually so serious that it required a visit to the local hospital. Some rumours suggest it was his pride, rather than his forehead, that had been most hurt. But even if he did flounce off in an artistic hissy fit, I partly understand. There he was, at the height of his fame and peak of his creativity, exposing his chest and expounding his republicanism in the penniless north of eighties Britain, and what happens? Some turnip-brain lobs a coin at him, a coin of the realm, bearing the image of the monarch. It was probably all too much.

'So do you want me to go?'

'NOOOOOOOOOOOOOOOOOOOOOOOOOOO.'

Cue guitars, drums, and a thunderous version of 'I Just Want to See the Boy Happy' complete with rotating orange lights, giving the set the look and feel of a serious road traffic incident or nuclear emergency. I think I'm hypnotized. I want to get closer. I want to inhale. I want to witness the damage, experience the contamination. Our man has also become more adept at dealing with projectiles over the years. During the evening, several plastic glasses come flying his way. As one approaches his face he doesn't duck but simply watches its trajectory until the last moment then lays his head on his shoulder and lets it sail past. When what looks like a bejewelled G-string arcs towards him, he nonchalantly catches it in his free hand and tosses it back to the audience. No turds are thrown, as far as I know. And no gladioli either, which is a bit of a surprise. In my final year at Portsmouth Poly, half a dozen of us would set off on a Friday or Saturday night in the direction of the Albert Tavern or the student union. On the way, we'd uproot all manner of vegetable matter (preferably flowers from private gardens or council roundabouts, though on one occasion a young conifer still in its root bowl, and on another night a bouquet from Southsea Cemetery – for which many apologies) and arrive in the bar like overcamouflaged deserters from a rather camp army. By the end of the night the dance floor would be strewn with petals and leaves. It was during this time that I preferred to think of my centrally heated flat in a comfortable hall of residence in central Portsmouth as 'a rented room in Whalley Range'. 'Oh Manchester, so much to answer for,' as somebody once said. In my case it turned out to be a prophecy rather than a backward glance. Two years at the university as a trainee probation officer. Eight years tramping around the estates and tower blocks *being* a probation officer. Twenty years hanging around outside Old Trafford trying to blag tickets. Five years at the *other* university teaching poetry. One especially satisfying afternoon in 1987 on the way to interview a prisoner in Strangeways, stopping in at Piccadilly Records to buy *Strangeways Here We Come*.

I wasn't at the famous non-gig in Preston myself. In fact the last time I saw Morrissey in the flesh was in 1984, 10 June, an open-air all-dayer in London's Jubilee Gardens to commemorate the dismantling of the GLC. The area now contains a posh hotel and an aquarium. 'Hello, we're the Smiths,' he said, and they kicked into 'Nowhere Fast'. Misty in Roots also played that day, and Hank Wangford and Billy Bragg, and so did the Redskins, the shaven-headed SWP band from York. During their set, the stage was invaded by East End bootboys in ankle-high Doc Martens, black Harrington jackets and braces hanging down by their knees. They were also carrying branches and sticks, though not in homage to the Smiths. It was a hot summer day. In the big crowd around the government buildings to either side of the stage, skirmishes and dust-ups flared all through the afternoon, leading to a pitched battle and bloodshed in the early evening. Since then it feels like Morrissey has never been far from physical violence, whipping up the far right at the infamous Finsbury Park gig by swathing himself in the Union Jack, extolling the art of pugilism on *Southpaw Grammar*, flirting with gang-culture and mobster imagery on *You Are the Quarry*, and on *Ringleader of the Tormentors* singing repeatedly of knifings and murders and revenge. At least once in tonight's performance he puts a two-fingered gun to his head or points it into the audience. Several times he makes a repeated stabbing gesture in the direction of either his heart or his groin or towards some imaginary enemy in front of him. During another mime, he draws an invisible blade across his open neck.

But enough about knives – let's talk about clothes. This is a four-shirt gig. The first is acid pink, satin, knotted at the bottom around his waist, and darkened by sweat after only two numbers. When he turns his back to the audience and fiddles with his midriff I have to assume he's retying the bow. But he's undoing the buttons. Steven Patrick Morrissey at forty-six years of age is taking off his pink satin shirt in the King George's Hall in Blackburn and hurling it into the crowd. The inevitable feeding frenzy takes place, but only in the corner of my eye. I'm staring at Morrissey, lead singer of the Smiths, with his waiter's hips and his builder's shoulders. I'm staring at his stomach. It isn't the toned and shaped and personally trained stomach of a Los Angeles resident. Neither is it the pie-and-chips pregnancy of the shirtless car-park attendant on an August bank holiday, or the space-hopper beer belly of the Newcastle United fan, stripped to his waist and standing on his seat in a howling north-easterly at St James's Park on New Year's Day. So what is it? It's sort of proud, sort of serious. It's very real. Back in the eighties, there was barely enough of Morrissey to stop his paisley shirts and floral blouses from completely imploding. Now he looks like a retired shire horse standing on its back legs, or something from mythology, as if those tailored Italian trousers might be hiding a pair of goat's legs. And above the trousers comes the stomach, and above that the chest. It's nakedness rather than nudity. It says *here I am*. Or it says *so what did you expect?* Or it says *if you're going to stab me, here's where you put the knife*.

'The Youngest Was the Most Loved' is riotous. 'I'll Never Be Anybody's Hero Now' is operatic, with Morrissey in a slow-motion bullfight with himself. Or with the microphone and its long flex, he's a lion-tamer. Of the Smiths' numbers, he sings 'Still Ill' and 'Girlfriend in a Coma'. To his left-hand side it should be Johnny Marr of course, but it's the very peculiar Boz Boorer, playing a double guitar in the colours of the Italian flag, and in another song playing two half-filled (i.e. half-empty) glasses of water with a teaspoon. However, it's during this piece, maybe three quarters of an hour into the show, that I suddenly realize how hooked I am, how completely engaged with the performance, and how moved. Morrissey is singing 'Life is a Pigsty' with its epigraphic, almost apologetic 'same old SOS' and its rain-swept background, a conscious echo of the deliriously sad 'Well I Wonder'. I'm having a moment, and it is only a moment, but for as long as it lasts I'm tied by the arms to two horses which gallop away in opposite directions, one towards a past I can never have again, and one towards the unavoidable misery of old age.

A little later I have another moment, but this time it's more powerful and lasts a lot longer. It begins with a reverberating, wuthering guitar sound, peaks on the line 'But you go and you stand on your own, and leave on your own, and you go home and you cry and you want to die,' and it ends with the crash of an enormous gong as Moz, with his carved head and crestfallen quiff, stands motionless, silhouetted within its trembling circumference. And let me make it clear that I haven't had a drink, because I'm driving, and nothing more powerful than a fruit pastel has passed my lips all evening, but forgive me, because I'm tearful. Morrissey's peculiar gift has always been to induce, in those people who allow him to, an overpowering sense of loneliness, and clearly I am susceptible to his spell. I'm a person whose mood indicator rarely swings below the contentment line and is more often than not up at the happiness end of the dial; I'm also standing hand in hand with the woman I love. But for the duration of this song, right through its six minutes and forty-four seconds, I feel abandoned and alone. I also feel a great tide of sympathy. Not for Morrissey: for all the pain and the guilt and the misery he tells us he's suffered, not once in the last two decades have I ever felt sorry for him, not for a split second. No, the person he makes me feel sorry for is myself.

There's an encore. 'Irish Blood, English Heart' goes down a storm with the thugs in the audience, attending tonight in the absence of a Premiership football fixture or an Oasis gig. Their fists are all in the air at once, each with an orange security band around the wrist. The bits of the song they appear to like best are those containing the word 'English'. They even sing about spitting at Oliver Cromwell though I suspect that if they knew what Cromwell had actually done in Ireland they'd be more likely to shake his hand than gob on his name. The band, in their Four Poofs and a Piano outfits, give a low bow with Mozzer in the middle, then Boorer makes a paper aeroplane out of the set list and launches it into the audience. Unfortunately I'm not under the flight path. Then it's all over. We spill out into the street, and stare at the people we have become.

It's midnight before we get back to Yorkshire. At Mum and Dad's we get a cup of tea before peeling the Tudge out of bed and driving home. For whatever reason, Dad's in a contrary mood.

'So who is it you've been to see?'

He knows.

'Morrissey.'

'Who's he then?'

He knows.

'He was in the Smiths.'

'And what did they ever do?'

He genuinely doesn't know the answer to this question, though he does know how much I liked them, and therefore that I'll protest too much and in all probability collapse under cross-examination. I can't believe I'm debating indie guitar music with my dad, but I've swallowed the bait and I am.

'They were only the most influential British guitar band of modern times, that's all,' I tell him.

'Rubbish,' says he. 'Everyone knows that only American bands are influential.'

'Oh, yeah, like who?'

There's a moment's silence while he takes a taste of his whisky and considers his reply. Then he says, 'The Eagles.'

The Blue Nile
Bridgewater Hall, Manchester
21 May 2006

Or rather Paul Buchanan, who is the Blue Nile by another name. In a prearranged assignation, we buy our tickets from a friend of a friend in a dodgy-looking boozer around the back of the venue. Our tout isn't attending himself, he's going to see Dinosaur Junior somewhere up the road. He points vaguely in the direction of Collyhurst or Cheetham Hill. The drinkers in here are in marked contrast with the clientele of the cafe-bar of the Bridgewater Hall. The men, in their black polo necks, look like subscribers to *Wire* magazine, and the women, with their scraped-back hair and little silver glasses, look like off-duty nuclear physicists. Or Christians.

The Blue Nile have recorded only four albums in twenty-two years. It's slow going, but not bad for a band who were only invited into the studio to road-test a digital recording console. Paul Buchanan thanks the audience for their loyalty and their patience. In the perfect acoustics of this purpose-built concert venue, the shouted compliments of the audience are just as audible as the amplified comments of the singer-songwriter, so a kind of dialogue develops, with respect flowing back and forth in either direction. One voice, after 'Because of Toledo', cries out, 'That song is amaaaaazing.' The frontman bows in gratitude then mumbles an unironic 'Thank you.' Throughout the performance he makes repeated enquiries about the quality of the sound, rather like a nervous poet asking the people at the back of the library if they can hear, and apologizes over and over again for his lack of expertise and stagecraft. It's either a great act – the kind of thing an ex-wife or disgruntled former band member finally blows the whistle on – or it could be that Buchanan is genuinely one of the most humane and humble people ever to put his lips to a microphone. Shiny with perspiration after one number, he eventually allows himself a small moment of self-consciousness, towelling himself down and saying, 'It's hard work being enigmatic.'

Over the years, I've realized that my record collection also functions as a kind of photograph album or diary. A lot of my memories are stored within it. Almost every song throws up an image, often something unremarkable or incongruous, probably connected to the first time I ever heard it. When I hear 'Are "Friends" Electric?' I'm working the scoreboard at Marsden Cricket Club, sitting under the eaves in the upper deck of the stone-built shed, with the smell of oily lawnmowers and cut grass below me and my dad marking out his run-up from the pavilion end. There must have been a radio on in the background. When I hear 'Warm Leatherette' by The Normal, I'm in Flix's nightclub in Huddersfield watching a girl on her own on the dance floor – she's mesmerizingly beautiful and entirely unobtainable. Killing Joke's 'Requiem' is the view at night from my bedroom, overlooking the village. The B-52's' 'Rock Lobster' is my sister and her mates in the bus shelter one evening, not their faces but the glowing tips of several Silk Cut cigarettes, like fireflies in the darkness. 'One Step Beyond' used to be my mate Wellie in a pork-pie hat, but that's been replaced by the image of his coffin at the front of the crematorium, draped with a Huddersfield Town flag. And for 'Tinsel Town in the Rain' by the Blue Nile I'm in the car, outside a friend's house, on a cinder track by the side of a mill. His neighbour had come to the door, complaining that a crappy orange Lada was occupying his parking place and could the owner please move it. I'd shouldered past him on the way out of the house, revved the engine loudly and spun the wheels on the unmade road as I manoeuvred that heavy, awkward slab of a car to the other side of the terrace. Crappy it certainly was but, for some inexplicable reason, it had come supplied with a stereo of a higher value than the vehicle itself, and a rather swanky automatic aerial that erected telescopically from the rear near-side when the ignition was fired. A song was playing on the radio and I liked the sound of it, so I sat there for another two or three minutes waiting for the DJ to announce the title and the name of the band.

It's concerned me, every once in a while, that listening to music from almost quarter of a century ago – or worse, going to see ageing bands still playing that music – makes me trapped in the past or out of touch. But it concerns me no longer. It doesn't bother people who listen to Beethoven, so why should it bother me? Also, a song might have been written *then*, but I'm listening to it *now*, right here, in the present moment. It's a contemporary experience; if it still sounds astonishing, why shouldn't I be engaged with it or excited by it? Or moved, deeply and intensely moved, as I am here, in the cathedral-like surroundings of the Bridgewater Hall and simultaneously back in the butterscotch-coloured Lada with the dust settling around the tyres and the engine slowing to a comfortable, idling purr.

José Carreras
Galpharm Stadium, Huddersfield
9 June 2006

Cancelled. Headline in the *Huddersfield Examiner*: 'No Way José'.

The Assassin Tree

It was Craig Raine who said librettists are to opera what toilets are to theatres. So when someone from the Edinburgh Festival asks if I'd be interested in writing the words for a newly commissioned opera, I pause: I've never thought of what I do as a mere functional necessity, and because of my surname I'm wary of all lavatorial connections. But in the end I can't say no. I've been writing song lyrics for four or five years now, usually for the docu-musicals I've been involved with but also for singers and bands such as Tom McRae or the Family Mahone. I'm also writing a book about music – this book – so any opportunity to collaborate with musicians or hang about backstage at a gig is not only irresistible but tax-deductible. And even though modern song lyrics and contemporary poems are very different things, I'm very much attracted to the notion that in ancient times the two things were almost inseparable, and might be so again at some stage in the future. Any possibility of getting poetry out from between the silent pages of a book and giving it a living voice is worth exploring.

I meet the composer, Stuart MacRae, in a nondescript cafe on a balcony above the recently sanitized and sterilized concourse of Manchester Piccadilly. Stuart is the bright young thing of the contemporary music scene, especially in his native Scotland. He's a serious guy with a wry smile, which I tend to think of as a winning formula, especially on a first date. We've arranged to meet and talk about ideas – to find common ground on the subject of art, I suppose – but we're really sniffing each other out. You can't truly collaborate with someone unless you like them, and after spending most of the day talking about a character called Waingro in the Michael Mann film *Heat*, I get the sense that things are going to be OK. In and amongst, we find out that we like narrative, that we like dramatic moments, that we admire beauty, and that it's always useful in a show of any kind if a ghost shows up at some point in the proceedings.

We also talk about music: what it is, and what it isn't. I put my cards on the table and tell him I've spent most of my life listening to music and I'm pretty clear about what works and what doesn't. I don't exactly quote Mark E. Smith: 'I've got a layman's ear: if it sounds rubbish to me, it's rubbish,' but I can hear his voice in the background. Having said that, as a resident of Huddersfield and an occasional attendee of its world famous Contemporary

Music Festival, my definition of what works can be fairly wide. I've been present during symphonies for twenty-five biscuit tins and solo trombone, or that type of thing, and sometimes I've laughed out loud, sometimes I've walked out, and sometimes I've been utterly stunned. So my understanding of music isn't just confined to tunes you can whistle in the bath.

You can't whistle Stuart's music in the bath – I think he would acknowledge this. Stuart's composition, it seems to me, is about texture and performance. It demands attention, and possibly because it is music that challenges and takes risks, the linguistic component deserves a kind of clarity and certainty. At least, when I put this to him he doesn't disagree. I'm also relieved to see him nodding when I express reservations about the use of contemporary dialogue in opera. It might be a risky statement, coming from a contemporary poet who rejoices in the modern idiom, and directed towards a contemporary composer who turns tradition on its head. But we seem to be in firm agreement that operas in which posh-sounding sopranos sing lines like 'Do you want pizza or a burger for tea, Kevin?' to which posh-sounding baritones respond, 'Don't worry, sweetheart, I'll get a pie in the boozer,' can only be comic or unbearably ironic, and we want to be more sincere than that.

This is the plan: I'll write the libretto first, then Stuart will set it to music. We've both read J. G. Frazer's classic study of magic and religion, *The Golden Bough*, at an impressionable age and we're keen to do something from the first section of that book. According to the legend, a priest or king guards Diana's sacred grove, but is stalked by would-be assassins intent on stealing his crown. In my libretto, as it takes shape, Diana becomes a fertility goddess or queen, to be protected and loved, and through the priest I begin to explore issues of survival, love and family ties. Also, you can't call a royal deity Diana these days without making particular allusions, but when I suggest to Stuart that we call one of the other characters Dodi he has some very serious misgivings. And he's probably right; a subtext should probably remain below the waterline, even if it has broken the surface of the writer's subconscious on more than one occasion. In terms of the text, I produce something fairly traditional, I think. The four characters speak to each other in a language that is somewhere between rhetoric and conversation. Rhymes and half-rhymes act as little connecting threads both within and between lines of dialogue, but there is no hard and fast metre. Once a lyricist fixes a phrase with a regular or insistent rhythm, any composer is hamstrung. Besides which, Stuart doesn't really do rhythm.

On reflection, collaboration is probably the wrong word for a project like this. I do my bit – it takes about three months, on and off – then I send it to Stuart, who works on it for over a year and a half. So even though it would be semantically incorrect to say so, the collaboration is all Stuart's. He has to make the words bend, he has to shape the noises around the language, he has to make things fit. The point is, I suppose, that as someone who can read and write, Stuart understands the bit supplied by me. But as someone who can't read music, can't play an instrument with any great proficiency, doesn't listen to much opera and has never worked on a libretto, my understanding of his contribution is always going to be limited.

And it's this business of taking a back seat (accidentally echoing Raine's metaphor here) that proves the most fascinating and liberating aspect of all. As a poet and a writer, I'm usually in charge. I take sole responsibility for the work, and apart from the odd editorial comment and advice from domestic sources, it's my show. This opera is definitely not my show. At an open workshop during the writing period, during which we rehearse a couple of sections with singers and a pianist, a well-meaning lady in the audience kindly points out that its working title, *The King of the Wood*, is . . . well, boring. A few months later I notice the opera is now called *The Assassin Tree*. At the same workshop we meet the prospective directors/ designers, Emio Greco and Pieter C. Scholten. At this point in the development of the opera, I imagine that some conversation with its author will be essential if the philosophy of the piece is to be properly visualized on stage. Like, are you picking up on the Diana reference, guys? But this is a conversation that never takes place. Because I'm not the author. Or am not perceived to be its creator, at any rate. I'm the librettist. Another example: the proposed cover image for the programme is to be a wonderful photograph of a gnarled and knotted old tree, washed in a coloured light. I'm asked if I prefer the red or the green. I say red. It's green.

On the night of the premiere, on a drizzly August evening in Edinburgh, I walk with Speedy Sue under a borrowed umbrella across slippery paving stones towards the

Lyceum. Even now, with only an hour to go, I still don't know what *The Assassin Tree* is *like*. But I'm looking forward to the curtain going up, when quite literally I'm just going to sit back and see, and hear, what happens.

Gigs

Offers of work so far this month:

As part of National Bread Week, Warburton's, 'the family bakers', would like me to nominate my favourite Yorkshire picnic site. If the region can identify as many 'hotspots' as possible, it might stand a chance in the Golden Slice Picnic Awards.

The Manchester Literature Festival is staging a Poetry Bed event in Heal's department store to tie in with this year's National Poetry Day theme of Dreams. Two poets will 'perform' in a four-poster bed in the ground-floor window. The letter says 'each poet will have three slots'.

A PR firm, pitching for a marketing campaign, wonder if I would like to be the new face of Tetley's Herbal Teas. My profile 'dovetails nicely' with Tetley's and I am very popular with their target demographic (thirty-five-to fifty-five-year-old poetry-reading herbal-tea-drinkers). Their products include Peppermint Punch, Summer Berry Merry and Camomile Smile.

And a couple from Japan have emailed to say they like my work so much they'd like to come and spend their honeymoon with me in my house.

Rock of Ages

As a poet, I'm supposed to be attracted to Bob Dylan as a lyricist. Even as a fellow poet. That's the received wisdom, and it's certainly true that I've come to Dylan through a series of recommendations and tips, nearly always from other writers. It was the poet Matthew Sweeney who first explained to me that *Highway 61 Revisited* and *Bringing It All Back Home* were the two albums I shouldn't be able to exist without, and as an example of Dylan's songwriting genius, went on to recite the whole of 'Gates of Eden'. He was word-perfect, give or take. And it was Glyn Maxwell who explained to me that the best of Dylan didn't stop with *Blood on the Tracks*. Arriving early at his house in Welwyn Garden City one morning, I sat on the front step listening to 'Don't Fall Apart On Me Tonight' from a steamy bathroom window, with Maxwell himself on backing vocals, his voice bouncing off the tiles, drowning out the doorbell. He also let me in on a fact that all Dylan fans have committed to memory. Namely, a man hasn't found true love until he finds the woman who will hang on to his arm the way Suze Rotolo hangs on to Dylan on the front cover of *Freewheelin'*. No one else will do.

To have grown up when Dylan was emerging as a musical icon must have been a compelling experience, and the spell that Dylan still casts over his most diehard fans goes back some forty years. The image that persists is not Dylan as he is now, a chewed-up and grisly old granddad, but the Dylan of the sixties. It's amazing how many people are still wearing that look. But because I arrived late, I feel neither possessed by him nor possessive of him. I wouldn't want to be Bob Dylan; I don't fancy him. If he came to the house one day looking for Dave Stewart and I was out, it wouldn't kill me. I have never asked what I can do for Dylan, only what he can do for me. He has to earn his place in my house, typically alongside some obscure collective drug-addled noiseniks whose first and only album was made for 200 quid in an outside toilet in Hebden Bridge (what *did* become of Bogshed?). So there he is, sitting on the shelves not between Bo Diddley and Duane Eddy, and certainly not betwixt Dryden and Eliot, but sandwiched by Dexy's Midnight Runners and Echo and the Bunnymen. It's in that field I position Dylan, in that company I rate him, and in that context I prefer to think about him.

★

When asked, I always say the first single I ever bought was by the Sweet, after witnessing the platinum-haired Brian Connolly (now deceased) and three other interchangeable glam rockers pouting their way through 'Blockbuster' on *Top of the Pops*. Dylan would have been thirty-two at the time and about to release the now-deleted *Dylan*. To an impressionable youngster looking for pin-ups and heroes, the choice between four glittery men in catsuits and stacker platforms, and some clapped-out folkie singing 'Mr Bojangles', wasn't even a toss-up. Besides, 'Blockbuster' had a siren wailing in the background. It had all the tension of a state of emergency, all the energy of a riot, all the oomph of a car chase and a blue flashing light. I didn't know what the song was about, even though I knew it by heart; I didn't even realize that 'block' was a verb and 'buster' was a bloke. But in reality, my first ever single was somewhat less impressive.

In Bridlington High Street in 1972, at the height of the power-cut season, my Uncle Eric left the engine of his Humber Hawk running as he popped into a hardware shop for a dozen candles, two hot-water bottles, a battery-operated torch and a gallon of paraffin. Returning to the car, he handed me a seven-inch circle of floppy blue plastic, a free gift with every purchase over two shillings. It was a record. A flexidisc, in fact, almost transparently thin, with grooves on one side only and the sponsor's logo in the middle. It was a song, sung to the original Fabulous Platters' tune, and it went like this:

♫

They asked me how I knew,
it was Esso Blue.

I of course replied,
with lower grades one finds,
the smoke gets in your eyes.

♫

It left a deep and lasting impression. As adverts are supposed to, I guess. It's not by accident that the other song I remember word for word from the same era is the

Hoseason's Boating Brochure commercial, performed against a backdrop of deckshoes and blazers on the Norfolk Broads. 'Sail boats, canal boats, and cruisers too, all Britain's waterways waiting for you . . .' More importantly, though, possession of the flexidisc allowed me access to that strange and rarely used contrivance, the record player. In our house, this took the form of a dusty old box containing what seemed to be a potter's wheel and windscreen-wiper arm with a needle at the end like a beggar's toenail. It was brought out at parties, but its main purpose was as a novelty piece. A suitcase that made music – what could have been more amusing than that? My father owned about a dozen records, including the double-A-side single 'The Great Pretender'/'Only You' by the aforementioned Fabulous Platters. The rest were long-players, some classical stuff (*Golden Guinea Family Classics*), easy listening (*Strolling with George Shearing*), songs from the shows (*Oklahoma!, High Society*) and the odd cracked or chipped seventy-eight. Plus a few things less easily categorized: Victor Borge, Paddy Roberts, a Tom Lehrer album, and Bob Newhart's *The Button-Down Mind Strikes Back!* I played all the albums over and over again, especially those last two. I loved the exactness of the language, and the timing, and the delivery. Trying unsuccessfully to remember the songs and the jokes proved to me that in telling a story, diction is everything, and that actions do not, in fact, speak louder than words. And, of late, I've come to think that aspirant poets could do a whole lot worse than listen to smart-mouthed entertainers and deadpan comics like Lehrer and Newhart. A lot worse. For example, my father also had some jazz records – Dave Brubeck, Duke Ellington, Ella Fitzgerald. I didn't get it at the time, and even though I've given it every chance, it's still the only form of music I actively dislike. Either it's splodgy and haphazard, or it's that finger-clicking, foot-tapping sort of jazz that idles and revs but never actually sets off. To me, jazz is the very opposite of poetry, especially Larkin's poetry, and his enthusiasm for it has always been a puzzle and an irritation. My least favourite night out in the whole world would be an evening of improvised poetry/jazz fusion in the smoky, stone-flagged cellar of a chain-owned wine bar. All saxophones should be rounded up and disabled.

There's no reason why my father shouldn't have been into Dylan, or at least owned one of his records. He could argue, I suppose, that he was too old, being in his late twenties when Dylan released his first album. Or too concerned with conveying his baby son back from the maternity ward a year later to worry about whether or not a hard rain was going to fall. Or too busy earning a crust by the early seventies to be shelling out good money on nonsense (or 'shit' as *Rolling Stone* magazine preferred) like *Self Portrait*. Also, photographic evidence from an earlier period shows my father to have been something of a Teddy boy, and in all likelihood, not readily disposed to such wispy-beardy acoustic musings. Add to this a history of working-class conservatism within the family, and the odds of a New World protest singer getting on the playlist in the family home were pretty slim. Tom Lehrer's line, 'The trouble with folk music is that it's written by the folk,' made my father laugh out loud, every time he quoted it.

So there was to be no Dylan for some time yet. Not even via my cousin, who was a few years older than me and listening to a lot of music. When I was thirteen, he played me *Animals*, the new Pink Floyd album. It had a pig floating above Battersea Power Station on the front cover, and obscenities on the lyric sheet, including the word 'fuck'. I was impressed. I took a paper round and saved up, and from an ugly shopping precinct in Ashton-under-Lyne bought what I still reckon to be one of the greatest rock albums of all time. I'd seen David Bowie on the telly singing 'The Laughing Gnome', and didn't know if he was a pop star or Tommy Steele. I'm not sure *he* knew at the time. Next time around, he was Major Tom, a spaced-out astronaut spiralling out of orbit, and a few years later, he splashed down as Ziggy Stardust, a bisexual alien with a buzz-saw guitar, come to save the earth. *The Rise and Fall of Ziggy Stardust and the Spiders from Mars* had been out five years by the time I bought it, but that didn't matter, because thirty years later, it still sounds like tomorrow. Bowie's transmutations, from androgynous alien to Thin White Duke to the synthesizer overlord of *Low* and *Heroes*, have always had the look and feel of something new, the 'next thing'. Dylan, by contrast, has always been retro, engaging with past models of songwriting and style. He wasn't the first folk singer, just as he wasn't the first man to pick up an electric guitar, or the first bluesman, pot-head, speed-freak or born-again God-botherer. At a time when Bowie was beaming in from another planet, on all sorts of levels, the earthbound Dylan was backtracking through images of Americana. Once again, it was a question of choice, between an exotic extraterrestrial on the one hand, and on the other, some dusty cowpoke in Stetson, corduroys and chaps.

My father, as it happened, was less keen on David Bowie than he was on Bob Dylan. As I walked through the living room with *Ziggy Stardust and the Spiders from Mars* under my arm, he pointed at it with the mouth-end of his pipe. 'What's that then?' And he'd obviously heard of the man and his music, because when I told him, he said, 'David Bowie? He's a homosexual.' Ten minutes later I flounced back through the living room and shouted, 'So what? Beethoven was deaf.' I wasn't allowed to play David Bowie on the record player, which of course made the music more thrilling, and his injunction led me further in the direction of subterfuge and deceit. The same year, I lied about my age and joined the Britannia Music Club of Great Britain, a mail-order organization, which offered an introductory package of four free albums on condition of purchasing at least one full-priced album per month for the next six months from their limited catalogue. With the right kind of guidance, I could have been listening to *Blood on the Tracks* or *Desire*. But I wasn't, I was listening to Black Sabbath, Deep Purple, Yes, Tangerine Dream and the like. All well and good in itself, but somehow . . . irrelevant. It was all wizards and warlocks, goat skulls, airbrushed dreamscapes and ruched purple blouses. There was something missing, and that something came my way about a year later, in the shape of punk. In the spirit the new era demanded (two purchases short of my contractual obligation and looking down the barrel of yet another gatefold-sleeved double concept album with a Dungeons and Dragons cover and mind-altered lyrics) I ripped up my membership card and told the Britannia Music Club to stick it where the sun don't shine.

I was fourteen in 1977, not really old enough or brave enough to be cropping my hair in the style of a Pawnee tribesman. I could hear the exhilaration of the songs and see the energy of the bands, but I needed punk to stay around for a while, to wait for me. If it had tailed off or petered out completely, it would have left me with nowhere to go, except back to Rick Wakeman or even away from music altogether. And obligingly, punk defied most of its critics, and also some of its own revolutionary statements, if not by continuing in its pure form, then at least by evolving in several different directions and producing music and bands that outlived the era and its ambitions. The first Undertones album, in 1979, was the one that eventually encouraged me to take all those Jethro Tull and Uriah Heep and various other troll-rock albums to the local tip and frisbee them into the path of an oncoming bulldozer. One Black Sabbath album, melted into a cone, actually made a very good vase, and some accompanying singles were morphed into ashtrays. John Peel was the root cause of this behaviour. Hour by hour, his ten-till-midnight slot on Radio 1 was edging out the satin-trousered leviathans of old with their fifteen-minute power ballads, in favour of demo tapes by so-called 'shambling' bands and other three-minute wonders, whose hearts were in the right place, even if their plectrums weren't. I recorded the show almost every night for two years. On one occasion, he played a whole side from the Clash's *Sandinista!*, not because he'd left the studio for a comfort break or a veggie kebab, but because *this was the stuff.* Pop and rock music would never be the same again – this time the cliché was true. Out of punk came the ska revival (bluebeat sung by punks), the mod revival (mod and soul sung by punks), post-punk (punks in over-coats) and the whole indie scene. Without punk, U2, REM, Oasis, Radiohead, Coldplay and a great number of other bands who are, or were, or will be the biggest band in the world, would never have happened. The rave and dance cultures of the past dozen years also descended from the punk movement and its attitude to music and society. Once again, if I try to slot Dylan into that environment and that atmosphere, he stands out like a dad at a disco. I can think of a particular gig, at Tiffany's, in Leeds' Merrion Centre, to illustrate the point. I'd gone to see Gang of Four, who were musical communists, or sociologists, or intellectuals at the very least. The line-up that night also included Pere Ubu, whose live album *390 Degrees of Simulated Stereo* was to songwriting what industrial noise pollution is to opera, and the Au Pairs, a feminist foursome, whose mantric refrain, 'We're equal, but different', was the chant of the evening. It was the early eighties by now, and this is what I wanted music to be. Antagonistic, apt, and original. To have heard Dylan, at that time, singing

> You know, a woman like you should be at home.
> That's where you belong,
> Watch out for someone who loves you true
> Who would never do you wrong

would have made my blood boil and my toes curl. 'Sweet-heart Like You' is a beautiful, beautiful song. I can hear that now. And I can see the gender politics of it more clearly, and hear the irony of some of the lines, and the playfulness, and the triangular tension between the song's paternalism, its protective instincts, and its sexual court-ship. But at the time, it would have jarred. Dylan's nation-ality would also have been a sticking point. It didn't matter that he'd spoken up for blacks, Jews, civil rights, the working man, the abused woman. According to the pre-vailing ideology, he came from a place whose name was a byword for bad taste. A country that was home to some of the most loathsome monsters of rock the planet had ever produced. A land that had seduced the likes of Lennon and Jagger and Bowie and sucked them dry of their credibility and talent. And somewhere that had broken free of the empires and commonwealths of old, only to impose its own economic and corporate imperial-ism on the world. 'I'm so bored with the USA,' barked Joe Strummer. 'They wouldn't let us into the USA, we didn't want to go there anyway,' sneered Sham 69's Jimmy Pursey, with adolescent glee.

That era also initiated the idea that any group or singer who grew in popularity could only be crap. For me, a band like Felt, who during one decade produced enough music to fill all my *Desert Island Discs* slots as well as my luxury item, had everything: shimmering songs, regular output, coolness beyond language, and a cult status bordering on universal obscurity. It didn't matter to me that all musicians from the beginning of time have wanted cosmic acclaim and record sales to go with it. As far as I was concerned, success implied treachery, and fame was betrayal.

It all amounted to a long and deep reluctance on my part, and a lingering hesitation that occasionally resurfaces as doubt. Should I really be listening to this guy? In the end, though, there is something inevitable about Bob Dylan. For me, 1984 was the turning point. Morrissey was going stale, Paddy McAloon was going soft, Ian McCulloch had gone over the top, Mark E. Smith was going through one of his phases, and my giro had just arrived. I'd heard *Slow Train Coming* at someone's house, and even though it banged on about Jesus and trundled forwards like the locomotive of its title, I thought there was something in it. I was also coming round to realizing that the days of turning up at a disco or club with a bunch of gladioli in my back pocket were numbered, and that not everyone wanted to hear 'Hexen Definitive / Strife Knot' on return from the pub. But it was more with a sense of exasperation and failure that I laid down 450 pence of taxpayers' money on *Another Side of Bob Dylan*. I don't know why I chose that record. I suppose from a credibility point of view, the fact that it was twenty years old made it more of a historical document / research project and therefore less problematic as a purchase. It even had a black and white cover to advertise its provenance. I couldn't rightly travel on public transport with the comic-strip artwork of *Shot of Love* about my person.

What I found amazing about the record was the narrative content, and also the humour. Did people actually do that? Punk had been all about slogans, and in the years that followed, lyrics had become a form of shorthand or subtitle to the experiences they described. I hadn't heard a record that told a story or made me laugh since 'Poisoning Pigeons in the Park'. But the music had an edge to it as well, an integrity that went beyond the klaxon harmonica and the knockabout words. Here was a storyteller pulling out all the stops – metaphor, allegory, repetition, detail. The songs themselves were written and performed to give the suggestion of spontaneity, improvisation even, but they were too memorable to be anything less than crafted and composed. I could quote them, and sing them, though without the original voice and the ditzy guitar work they lost a great deal in the translation. In all, I had the impression of someone totally aware of his talent and totally in control of his work. I've often argued that the only skill any writer needs is the ability to see his or her work from the other side. That is, to put him or herself in the position of the reader. Musicians must be able to do something similar, and I got the instant impression with Dylan that he knew exactly how he sounded in my ears.

1984 was also the year I started writing poetry. I wouldn't claim that there's any connection, that listening to Dylan made me want to write, or that his songs influenced my writing style. But I do think his lyrics, even at that early stage, alerted me to the potential of storytelling and black humour as devices for communicating more serious information. And to the idea that without an audience, there is no message, no art. His language also said to me that an individual's personal vocabulary, or idiolect, is their most precious possession – and a free gift at that. Maybe in Dylan I recognized an attitude as well, not more than a sideways glance, really, or a turn of phrase, that gave me the confidence to begin and has given me the conviction to keep going. Oh, yes, and there were poem-looking things on the back of that album, Beat-style Skeltonic-type things, but they were rubbish.

My collection grew very slowly. I was still more interested in new music than in the old stuff, and Dylan had associations. For example, at university, the only people I knew who listened to him were the two Druids on the eighth floor of Bateson Tower who grew weed on their window-sill and conducted business through their letter box. Five years later, Dylan was still prohibitively unfashionable, and by now I was a decent person with a proper job. So even when I rescued *Desire* from round the back of a settee in the Probation Service waiting room in Oldham, it was a couple of months before I gave it a spin. It was a great album, great tunes, but what was he wearing around his neck – a beaver? A bear? I didn't approve of the skin trade, at the time, and the barmy sleeve notes should have warned me against buying Ginsberg's *Journals* so many years later.

The trail could have gone cold at this stage. Very slowly I was getting the drift, and yet the sheer choice of material (twenty-four albums by now, not including live stuff, compilations and rarities) was both overpowering and off-putting. Left to my own devices I might have ended up with *Empire Burlesque*, and that would have been it. Finally, a friend had to intervene. A Dylan anorak of the first order, I don't think he could stand it any longer. Like there was something very obvious I needed to know, a sort of 'Bob Dylan birds-and-the-bees' conversation that needed to be had. He taped me *Blood on the Tracks* and *Blonde on Blonde*, and handed them over in a plain brown envelope. I played one in the car on the way to work, then knocked off early to listen to the other on the way home. And suddenly it all made sense. A few years later he taped me the *Bootleg Series, I–III*, on three cassettes, which I gave away to some big-eyed down-at-heel student in Lodz, Poland. It wasn't intended as the patronizing East–West gesture it probably looked like; neither was it a pure, altruistic act of Dylan-Aid. In truth, I'd bought the boxed CD set a few months earlier. I was, by this time, something of a fan, ranging forward and back through Dylan's output, having bought the necessary periodicals and biographies to map out the route. In fact there's an odd inversion within the strata of my record collection (as I still call it) whereby the oldest stuff is in the latest format, and the more recent stuff, up to a certain high-water mark, is on crackly vinyl. Which means Dylan actually sounds more alive than David Byrne, or Paul Weller, or Momus. It makes judging between them distinctly unfair.

I still haven't got everything he's done. I'm taking it slowly, because I think my appetite for his work is still growing. Also, to find myself in possession of the entire works of Bob Dylan, like owning every copy of *National Geographic* or a complete set of *Pokemon* cards, suggests to me a kind of autism that, for most of my adult life, I've been attempting to avoid. So I'm taking my time. Looking forward to it.

★

In the spring semester of 2000 I was teaching at the University of Iowa's Writers' Workshop, and heard that Dylan was playing at Cedar Rapids, an airport town a few miles up the road. Iowa City being something of an intellectual enclave within a landscape of corn, spuds and hogs, I thought a ticket might be hard to come by, but at the last minute, one landed in my pigeonhole.

I'd never seen Dylan live. It's the baby boom generation who seem most loyal to his cause, turning up to concerts year after year, agreeing in the rain afterwards that, yes, this was probably the worst ever, worse even than the one before, or the one before that. Then arranging to meet at the next gig. But the fanaticism isn't exclusive to that age band. Over the years, Dylanism has caught on amongst following generations, and academia has been one of its breeding grounds. Bob Dylan appears to be the musician of choice among the teaching staff of many an institute of further education. It's quite possible to hear his lyrics being bandied around in the senior common room, amidst discussions of prosody and symbolism. Mention of his name signifies a dignified and recherché understanding of popular culture, but nothing as crass as an interest in pop music or rock and roll. On some very basic level, it's a man thing. I don't listen to much Joni Mitchell myself, but from the times I have, I know she's a talented guitarist, that her compositions and orchestrations are extremely complex, that her lyrics are of a consistently high standard, and that she can sing a bit too. Sound like anyone else we know? She came out of the same folk-rock background not long after Dylan, but I don't see Joni on the syllabus.

Looking at the crowd from the middle-back of the Five

Seasons Center that night, I was amazed at the demographic spread. From ponytailed pensioners at the top end, to a baby in a papoose at the other. In between were locals, homeboys, farmers, bikers, crusties, rastas (white and black), groupies, roadies, slackers, civvies – the most diverse group of human beings I'd ever seen under one roof. Although the one thing that did unite them was dope. Even the farmers looked stoned.

Dylan was quite something. In his Zorro outfit, he played for almost two hours, with an appetite and enthusiasm for the songs that defied logic, given the thousands of times he must have sung and played them. In a move that typifies my approach to research, I wrote the set list on the bottom of a wax-coated drink holder, the surface of which rubbed off in my pocket on the way home, and with it the ink. But there are internet sites dedicated to such things, so I can confidently report that he played 'Desolation Row', he played 'Mama, You Been on my Mind', he played 'Gotta Serve Somebody', he played 'Tombstone Blues', he played 'I'll Be your Baby Tonight', he played 'Leopard-Skin Pill-Box Hat' and he played 'Tangled Up in Blue' (acoustic). The encore included 'Like a Rolling Stone', 'Knocking on Heaven's Door', 'Don't Think Twice, It's All Right', and finished with 'Rainy Day Women #12 & 35'. I didn't need the website to remember the sight and sound of a thousand or so stoners, stomping to their anthem, singing along with the man himself, under a swirling cloud of exhaled dope. It was the stuff of writing. Dylan was poetic – not the words themselves, I could hardly hear them – but the whole thing, the spectacle as it happened, and the image that remains.

The man in the next seat kept looking at me and shaking his head, like, 'I can't believe this guy has written all these songs.' I kept looking at Dylan's feet. He was hopping from one to another, like someone with shin splints or suffering from a circulatory problem. It was only towards the end of the evening I realized he was dancing.

Last FM

The Boy Smith, my technology guru, has installed some bewildering piece of software on my computer which means everything I play on iTunes is reported on the internet. Advertising your musical preferences to the whole of the universe and assuming someone out there might be interested requires a certain amount of arrogance, and like all forms of arrogance it has its dangers. Just as a hypothetical example, if you're being an irresponsible football-watching dad on a Saturday lunchtime, and you fob your daughter off by telling her that as long as she leaves you in peace for another forty-five minutes she can play on the computer, you could well log on to your website on Monday morning to find your current top-four playlist is recorded as follows: 'Making Your Mind Up' by Buck's Fizz, 'Axel F' by Crazy Frog, 'Last Christmas' by Wham! and the theme tune to *Byker Grove*. That's just a hypothetical example, obviously.

Mule Train

♫

VIRGO:
ALL ABOARD THE MULE TRAIN!
ALL ABOARD THE MULE TRAIN!

ANNIE:
So a friend of mine says honey
you can make some easy money
but my husband says No.

So I tell him that it's cushy
be a man don't be a pussy
and we give it a go.

So we're through the Channel Tunnel
but we're running into trouble
down at Waterloo.

'Cos they're calling back my darlin'
and there's half a K of Charlie
in his training shoe.

ALL:
Muling it muling it nation to nation.
Muling it muling it station to station.

PRISON GUARD:
But there's something in your luggage if we're not mistaken.
HMP final destination.

CELINE AND NATASHA:
She was studying her papers
she was working as a waitress
up in Amsterdam.

So we're happy little sisters
when we meet some dodgy misters
with a master-plan.

We're not mules but we were fools
we agreed to take some jewels
via London town.

They were tablets he was lying
she was laughing I was crying
when they sent us down.

ALL:
Muling it muling it nation to nation.
Muling it muling it station to station.

PRISON GUARD:
But there's something in your luggage if we're not mistaken.
HMP final destination.

CHARMAINE:
So I'm over in Jamaica
with my mother in the summer
when the telephone rings.

And the gunmen come and take me
and they lay me down and make me
do some terrible things.

When a brother puts his jigger
in your mouth and cocks the trigger
you don't shake your head.

So you carry out a mission
then you finish up in a prison
or you wake up dead.

VIRGO:
You can mule it in a boat
You can mule it in your coat
You can mule it on a plane
You can mule it on a train
You can mule it overland
You can mule it in your hand
You can mule it in a car
You can mule it in your bra
You can mule it in your booze
You can mule it in your shoes
You can mule it in your gut
You can mule it in your butt
You can mule it in a sack
You can mule it in the back
You can mule it in the front
You can mule it in your cu—

ALL:
Muling it muling it nation to nation.
Muling it muling it station to station.

PRISON GUARD:
But there's something in your luggage if we're not mistaken.
HMP final destination.

♫

Sung and performed by the inmates and wardens of HMP
Downview's Contract Services building for the film *Songbirds* (Century Films / Channel 4, 2005).

Star Sign

The high point around here is West Nab. It forms the elevated rump of a saddle-shaped feature that stretches across the moorland landscape between Marsden and Meltham and forms part of the Pennine watershed. I grew up in the shadow of Pule Hill, which West Nab looks down on. My dad once told me that Pule Hill was five million and sixty-one years old. 'How do you know?' I asked. He said, 'Because your granddad told me it was five million years old, and that was in 1946.'

West Nab and Pule Hill are only six miles apart; in over forty years I've got a little bit higher but not much further. About once a month I walk up to the top of the Nab. From my back door it's an hour's journey, and about half that time on the way back down. The path up the hill crosses Wessenden Head Road near the Cock Crowing Stone, a diamond-shaped rock pointing heavenwards, on to which some literalist, in white gloss, has painted the words 'Cock Crowing Stone'. I don't know the legend of the Cock Crowing Stone, but if you scramble to the top of it and shift your weight around you can rock it back and forth, like a big loose tooth. Red grouse mumble and burble down in the grass, or occasionally burst from underfoot and flap away, low and long across the moor. The other birds are meadow pipits, which sing out as they ascend then parachute back towards earth.

The head of West Nab is a heap of giant boulders, gouged and sculpted by the wind. The air up there is fast and sharp. There's almost a pattern to the boulders – it's almost a henge, but not quite. At some point in history, smaller stones have been cut into blocks and used to build a fold or a pen. Maybe it had a roof at one time, but it's just a couple of walls now. Other signs of human activity include the chiselled graffiti; these obstinate outcrops must have blunted the blade of many a knife over time. One rock simply carries the word 'MAJOR'. And there's a concrete OS trig point close to the summit, pointing north. One day last summer I came up here and was staring absent-mindedly out over the ranks of hills, looking north-north-east, when a further peak came into view. By further, I mean further than anything I'd seen before, and beyond the familiar landscape. I unrolled a map in my head and worked out that it had to be Ingleborough, that formidable and dramatic stump of a hill, like a limestone head wearing a cap of millstone grit, jutting nearly two and a half thousand feet into the heavens. About forty miles away, as the crow flies. I'd always thought of Ingleborough as belonging to some other view – someone else's territory, not part of this domain. And the appearance of a new mountain in your back garden can be a little bit disconcerting, especially when you've become so comfortable in your own surroundings and so confident of your local reference points.

Standing on top of West Nab, I can look out across a huge circumference of inspiration and influence. Starting westwards it's Manchester and Lancashire, so it's Joy Division and The Fall, it's the Smiths and Elbow, it's Magazine and the Buzzcocks and the Happy Mondays, it's the Chameleons, it's the Stone Roses, it's Oasis (before they became their own tribute band), and beyond them, out towards the Mersey, it's the Bunnymen and the Teardrop Explodes. Music, like the weather, always seemed to come from the north-west, and still does, carried on the prevailing breeze, perhaps. And occasional airwaves drifted in from the south as well, from Sheffield, which for me will always be the Comsat Angels, and maybe Pulp, and the odd track from the Human League, and maybe Arctic Monkeys, if they keep it up. After Sheffield it's more about the eye than the ear. Next it's Barnsley, which is *Kes*. Then it's the Yorkshire Sculpture Park, which is Barbara Hepworth as a young girl in Wakefield, watching the dark horizon from the back seat of her father's car. And *The Wakefield Mystery Plays*. And Bill Nelson and Be-Bop Deluxe, at a pinch. Keep revolving further and a line of cooling towers stretches directly east towards the coast, at full steam, warships heading for sea. Out there it's the vast Humber, swollen with the rain from this very hill, and it's Larkin and Marvell, then Ayckbourn higher up the shore. Leeds is Bennett and Harrison and Henry Moore – I can see the white tower of the Parkinson Building from here – and Bradford is Hockney and Priestley, and turning further still there's a line of wind turbines on the escarpment above Haworth, which is Brontë country. And a few more degrees brings Mytholmroyd and Hebden Bridge and Heptonstall into the picture, which is Hughes. And which is Plath. Then I'm back where I started from, full circle, looking north. Wordsworth, maybe, on a clear day, if the eyes could see that far.

There are thousands of other stars beyond this circle, in every direction, all worth setting a course for, some of them many times brighter. But these are the stars I tend to steer by – the constellation closest to home. You can't choose your place of birth. It's given. But in the great wheeling Zodiac of the world, this nameless northerly arc revolving around the rocky spindle of West Nab is the sign I'm happy to have been born under.

The Smiths
Huddersfield
8 January 2007

Listening to *Meat is Murder* on iTunes in the back bedroom when Speedy Sue shouts up the stairs, 'How do you want this steak cooking?'

On The Road 9

A reading in a cinema complex in Sheffield for the Off the Shelf Festival, followed by a Q & A session on contemporary poetics and related literary topics:

> Me: OK, one last question.
> Man: In a fist fight between you and Jarvis Cocker, who'd win?
> Me: Er . . . I've never met him, but from the pictures I've seen I'd have to fancy my chances.
> Man: He's outside.

On the Road 10

Poetry Live is the brainchild of Simon Powell. Simon's a grafter and an entrepreneur. He's been a lecturer in Hertfordshire, a car importer in Burnley, a bus driver in Yorkshire, and now he promotes poetry wherever and whenever anyone will let him. *Poetry Live* started as a couple of readings here and there, and now consists of over forty conferences a year from Plymouth to New-castle, from Preston to Brighton. It started with audiences of a couple of hundred in a function suite or a lecture room, and these days it isn't unusual for two and a half thousand to turn up, in big venues such as Westminster Central Hall, the Shaftesbury Theatre or the Bridgewater Hall in Manchester. The people who attend are mainly GCSE students and their teachers. On paper it should be a disaster. If the press are to be believed, today's fifteen-year-olds are knife-toting, dope-smoking illiterates with the concentration span of an aquarium fish; put a couple of thousand of them under one roof and goad them with poetry, and the result should be chaos. But against all the odds and against every expectation, it works. It's a kind of miracle. And by virtue of his brother's donated bone marrow, so is Simon Powell.

For some of the other poets and speakers on the schedule, getting back to Mid Wales or Tyneside is a problem to which a guest house and full English breakfast is the only solution. But by a strange quirk of geography and despite the gridlocked motorway system and the unintegrated rail network, it is logistically possible, just, to leave any town or city in the country in the late afternoon and arrive back in West Yorkshire before last orders. So I'm on the road a lot. Or I'm on the train. Most mornings between mid-November and late January, I'm like the business executive in a seventies sitcom who shaves in the car on the way to work. (Is that illegal? It's electric – not a soap-brush and cut-throat razor.) Or I'm the sleepy silhouette on the platform at Wakefield Westgate buying a sausage roll for breakfast before dawn. Or I'm the even sleepier silhouette stumbling around in the creepy long-stay car park at Wakefield Westgate after dusk, trying to remember where he parked his car. It's the closest I'll ever get to being on tour.

With thousands of students and half a dozen poets aiming to converge on one location each day, the statistical likelihood of a cock-up would seem pretty high. But either by goodwill, or good luck, or by the grace of a benevolent deity who deems poetry to be a virtuous activity on which fortune must smile, the operation runs fairly smoothly. Except perhaps for that time in Leeds Town Hall when I was snoring in the cloakroom when I should have been on stage. And perhaps that time at Liverpool Olympia, the day after a boxing match, when the walls of the dressing room were smeared with blood. And that time in Basildon, when I should have been in Basingstoke. And Cambridge, when I should have been in Oxford. Or that time on the way to Plymouth when the train seemed to be suffering from a kind of mechanical

ME, and according to the conductor lacked the energy to climb the Devon Bank, whatever that might be, and drew wearily to a halt outside Exeter. And in Norwich when I thought I had walked on to the stage but had walked into the orchestra pit. And that time in a sports centre in Brentwood when I sat for almost an hour among the jockstraps and support bandages of some of Essex's week-day athletes before convincing myself that in all likelihood I was not in the correct dressing room for the poetry reading. And that time in Braintree. I can't speak with authority about Braintree and its reputation, but in a list of places well known for their conferencing facilities, such as Birmingham or Harrogate or San Diego, Braintree does not figure highly. In fact there'd been some mix-up with the booking, and instead of being allocated a hall or a theatre, the venue for the day was a showjumping arena. The 'green room' was a glass-fronted judging box on the balcony, and to make our way to the podium we had to trot across a floor strewn with sawdust and straw. The smell of horses and their horsy habits never quite left the air, and it was so cold that one student turned blue and passed out. Flash-heaters – like afterburners from the space shuttle *Columbia* – were wheeled in at half-time. During my session I tried to make a joke about hoping to get away with a clear round, but no one could hear a word above the roar of the heaters. I even wore a rosette I'd found under a table, but I guess when you're close to freezing and all you can smell is manure and all you've got to look forward to for the next six hours is poetry, a rosette is not so hilarious after all.

It's not unusual for me to experience some kind of déjà

vu on the *Poetry Live* circuit – to walk out on to a stage and feel that I've been here before. Then to realize I have, but on the other side of the footlights, ages back, watching a band. Prefab Sprout at St George's Hall, Bradford. Bauhaus at Portsmouth Guildhall. The Clash at Leicester De Montfort Hall. My most vivid flashback comes at Guildford Civic Hall, where I saw Echo and the Bunny-men some time in the early eighties. It's a gig I remember not for the quality of the performance but because later that night the driver of the National Express coach from London to Portsmouth decided not to open the door of his vehicle to the half a dozen Bunny-people in Guildford bus station, and with a puff of exhaust fumes and a squeal of rubber shot off along the A3. Me and a friend and four other people in combats and moccasins spent the small hours being turfed out of shop doorways on the chintzy high street by the police and finally bedded down in the A & E department of the local hospital. I told them I'd got a broken finger and fortunately the waiting time was so long they never got around to checking. Twenty or so years later I walk out from the wings and I remember the angular architecture and the wooden panelling and the low stage. And because I'm high on nostalgia, or because I had to leave home at five thirty this morning and I'm hyper with coffee, I start singing. I sing, 'Won't you come on down to my rescue?' There's no response from the audience so I sing it again, 'Won't you come on down to my rescue?' a bit louder. Still no response. Then I look out at their blank, innocent faces – like a thousand eggs, not one of them cracked or broken – and do a quick bit of mental calculation. Obviously they weren't born when

Echo and the Bunnymen first started up. Or when they split up. But the fact that they still weren't born by the time the Bunnymen re-formed is the part that really shocks. Echo and the Bunnymen – a modern band. Echo and the Bunnymen – the band who come to mind when someone asks me if I've been listening to anything new. Who still sound to me like the here and now, and occasionally like the future.

There were no more *Poetry Live* events at Guildford Civic Hall after that because the following year the venue was earmarked for demolition.

*

At the end of each reading, students or teachers get a chance to ask questions. Sometimes there's a roving mic doing the rounds, so it's a bit like *Oprah*, and sometimes they just have to bellow their enquiries from the back of the stalls or the front of the balcony. Most of the questions relate to the poems on the exam, but there is a sizable minority of students whose curiosity is not yet guided by literary theory and whose confidence is not yet tempered by embarrassment. I like those students; they respond personally to the poems, which is refreshing, because that's the spirit in which the poems were written. So they'll say, 'I really liked that poem because it reminded me of my Auntie Barbara.' The fact that the poem is actually about a tractor or a tree doesn't really matter – a connection has been made and that's enough for the time being. Then there are the true oddballs and the cheeky monkeys. A young man in Newcastle waited patiently for ten minutes with his hand in the air before asking me who invented the dishwasher. Another time, *Poetry Live* was taking place in the faded and hushed surroundings of Lancaster's Ashton Hall. Before coming on stage, the chairperson for the day had given me a little introduction and also explained that during the break there would be a stall at the back selling crisps and Mars bars and the like. I finished reading the poems and asked if anyone had any questions. A boy at the back shouted out, 'How much are the Mars bars, mister?'

That's the way to do it, kid.

*

Once, at the same venue, I was hanging around in the dressing room either before or after the reading – I don't recall which. The room was hot and stuffy, and the painted-up windows wouldn't open, and a large moth, like a wind-up toy, was battering the pane. Not wanting to catch this angry, thrumming, hairy creature in my bare hands, I looked in a nearby cupboard, and amongst the candles and mop heads found an opaque glass lampshade about the size of a goldfish bowl – ideal for the job. I trapped the moth, intending to slide a book or a folder over the hole and carry it to the fire escape and release it into the breeze. But my phone rang. Or I was called on stage. Or someone wanted a book signing. So I put the lampshade down on the windowsill with the moth inside it, thinking I'd be back in a moment or so.

Time speeds up as you get older, everyone agrees. Take your eye off the clock for a moment and the seasons slip past. Lapse into a routine and the months fall like dominoes. When I return to the dressing room, the windowsill is covered in dust, and beneath the glass lampshade, within a circle of polished wood, there's a dead moth, perfectly preserved, completely intact. A year has gone by. I poke at the dry, papery creature with the end of my finger, and of course it doesn't move. But like the unexpected and uncomfortable recollection of something I'd told myself not to forget, it suddenly lifts and flutters and comes furiously alive in my head.

A Few Facts in Reverse Order

♪

Ten – they peep through the spyhole, bang on the door.
Nine – I slept for a year on my cousin's floor.
Eight – you can lean on your mop for two hours a day.
Seven – only amnesia takes the past away.
Six – pinstripe and denim are this year's black.
Five – the cops thought I'd been slashed by a wild cat.
Four – one man's life is another man's razor.
Three – they sent me away for skew-whiff behaviour.
Two – I once stole ice from the London marathon.
One – they watch me at night, I'm the nightwatchman.

He once stole ice from the London marathon.
We watch him at night, he's the nightwatchman.

Ten – I can bend a car door with my bare skin.
Nine – it takes exactly eleven minutes to swing.
Eight – you can't choose your family but you can choose your
    visitors.
Seven – I was manhandled once by babysitters.
Six – prison is a disease called boredom.
Five – I take snapshots of the cars I've stolen.
Four – one man's sheet is another man's rope.
Three – you can lose your footing on lino and soap.

Two – you can't overdose on two paracetamol.
One – they watch me at night, I'm the nightwatchman.

He can't overdose on two paracetamol.
We watch him at night, he's the nightwatchman.

Ten – my dad's waiting for his third heart attack.
Nine – my auntie's got six months to live, if that.
Eight – you wear your heart in your shirt pocket in this place.
Seven – a supper fit for a king is a Jaffa Cake.
Six – I'd never top myself, that's just madness.
Five – these cuts you see are from roses and brambles.
Four – prison is the drip, drip, drip of a ping-pong ball.
Three – prison is the pip, pip, pip at the end of a phone call.
Two – your watch goes slow when it's clocking your lifespan.
One – they watch me at night, I'm the nightwatchman.

His watch goes slow when it's clocking his lifespan.
We watch him at night, he's the nightwatchman.

♫

Sung by Robin in the film *Feltham Sings* (Century Films/
Channel 4, 2002).

The Wedding Present
Holmfirth Picturedrome
31 March 2007

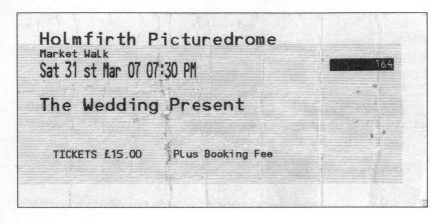

Holmfirth Picturedrome
Market Walk
Sat 31 st Mar 07 07:30 PM

164

The Wedding Present

TICKETS £15.00   Plus Booking Fee

It's just some boy,
probably dressed in corduroy.
He grew up fast but you've not changed at all.

'Corduroy', the Wedding Present

All good things come to those who wait. Keep following a band for long enough, and eventually they'll be playing in a nearby village. You might not be able to get a ticket to see Arcade Fire or the Killers right now, but if you're patient, one day they'll be appearing in your local working men's club or church hall. Twenty years ago I might have travelled half the length of the country to see 'everybody's second favourite band' the Wedding Present, even without a ticket; tonight, it's like they've come to see me. We don't even leave the house until seven forty-five, but that isn't because we're being fashionably nonchalant, it's because the babysitter hasn't arrived.

At any gig, most crowds develop a familiar sort of structure. This isn't always apparent from a position on the ground, but from the balcony of Holmfirth Picturedrome (rather worryingly held up with builders' props rather than some more traditional form of architectural support) the observer gets a very clear picture of the phenomenon. Let's start at the front, and with those people at the very front, and let's call them 'fronters'. Fronters get to a gig very early, walk straight towards the stage and remain there for the rest of the evening. They don't drink very much because going to the bar would mean forsaking their position, something they are not prepared to consider. The fronters' place at the very front is non-negotiable, and unlike other places within the crowd they have something solid and fixed to hold on to, which makes them hard to dislodge. They are a single line, one person deep. They appear to be privy to all kinds of inside information and arcane knowledge, such as the bass player's nickname, and will occasionally call out for an obscure B-side, which among their own ranks (that is to say the front rank) is a CULT CLASSIC. They don't dance and tend not to sing along either, but prop their elbows on the front of the stage and gaze upwards. Titbits and mementos occasionally come their way, such as a plectrum, a broken drumstick, or that holy grail – the set list. And to crown their achievement they get the one thing denied to most other people at the gig, i.e. an

uninterrupted view of the lead singer's choice of footwear. So to the uninitiated, fronters appear to be afficion-
ados or part of an in-crowd, but in actual fact they
are stalkers. Band members, I've noticed, treat them
with a certain amount of caution, tending to avoid eye
contact and preferring to banter with the anonymous
mass of the audience further back in the hall. From
on stage, they must look like non-swimmers at the
deep end, clinging hold of the edge of the pool, and to
reach out to save them would be to get dragged in and
to drown.

But as creepy as they are, fronters have a useful function, in that they provide a barrier of soft tissue between
the rigid edge of the stage and the next section of the
crowd – the moshers. In fact the mosh pit is a community
within a community and has a structure of its own, with
a hard core of participants forming the main nucleus and
lighter or less stable elements towards its outer edge. I've
sometimes imagined that at the very centre there's a kind
of sweet spot, like the eye of the storm, around which
everything else revolves, a position of almost Buddhist-
like tranquillity. But if it exists I've never found it. The
mosh pit is an energized entity fuelled by excitement and
adrenalin, and not always a pleasant place to be, though
most moshers appear to abide by an unwritten code of
practice that might be described as a kind of gentlemen's
anarchy. Stage-divers will always be caught, crowd-surfers
will always be rolled, and anyone who slips or stumbles
will always be hoisted back to their feet. I've also noticed
a discreet form of gallantry in the mosh pit, whereby
female moshers are allowed a few more centimetres of

personal space to perform their gyrations and are man-handled with greater sensitivity.

A gap tends to open up around the mosh pit – a sort of dry moat or buffer zone – and in my experience, this arc of no-man's-land is the most dangerous area of any gig. A combination of both the ripple effect and chaos theory are at work here: as it radiates outwards, the knock-on effect of any disturbance becomes magnified and exaggerated as it travels, so that a relatively innocuous push or shove within the tightly packed core can result in the slewing and spilling of several bodies at the circumference. It's also a zone inhabited by the unconfident or inexperienced mosher, who is a danger to both themself and others. But the main peril comes from the people on the other side of the moat, those who henceforth shall be referred to as the firemen. The firemen like PROPER MUSIC, not this kind of stuff, but have come to the gig because the venue has a late licence and anyway they're on the day shift so have been asleep all day and now want SOMETHING TO DO. They've gravitated towards the front of the venue because they're NOT SCARED, and as well as being tough they're also big, because they WORK OUT, and they don't like people coming too close, let alone pushing past. So with their pints clasped against their chests and their girlfriends manfully protected beneath their sizable shoulders, they form a semicircular wall of muscular flesh, through which very few enter and very few leave. Moshers who are thrown across the moat in their direction can expect to be propelled back at twice the speed, because even though moshing looks violent it is not PROPER FIGHTING.

If the crowd at a gig can be thought of in anatomical terms, with the fronters and moshers as the scalp and the head and the firemen representing the neck or collarbone, then the torso is made up of an amorphous mass, the 'trunkers', whose density and enthusiasm is greatest in the upper chest area and dwindles towards the rear end. There's no real defining characteristic here, although the reaction from this anonymous majority will usually determine the success of a gig. The fronters might be leaning forward to touch their idols, and the moshers might be leaping like salmon, and even the firemen might be tapping their toes, but unless the event meets with the general approval and collective appreciation of the trunkers, it's a failure. They are the gig-going equivalent of the middle classes, and no election can be won without them. Sometimes little pockets of action or anomalous behaviour are discernible within this mass: a weirdo dancer whose limbs are moving to the beat of a different drum, a howling drunk shouting at the ceiling, or further back, where the crowd starts to thin out, someone sitting on the floor, or a couple in honeymoon mode, or a couple having a blazing row. Beyond them, in the far nether regions of the venue, come the drinkers, the dealers, and a whole bunch of folk whose relationship with the actual music is entirely peripheral. If a dog is to be found, or a mother and toddler, or coach driver eating a pie, or someone playing a slot machine, or someone asleep, or a game of football, it will probably be in this hinterland where the sound of guitars clashes with the chatter of bouncers and bar staff. Where the warm yellow glow of the stage lights ends and a cold, fluorescent brightness begins. The promoter and his henchman sit behind a counter like Fagin and Uriah Heep unashamedly counting out tenners and stacking coins into numerically significant piles. In the upstairs bar a couple of guys are reading the paper, a few more are absorbed text-messaging, and on the two precarious-looking wings of the balcony (the arms), furnished not only with chairs but with comfy old settees, come those who have elected to sit rather than stand and to see rather than hear. This includes our party, until the first few chords of 'My Favourite Dress', at which point an altercation with the firemen becomes inevitable.

Full of people, the venue looks smaller and more intimate than it did earlier in the day, when it was just a draughty, empty hall echoing with the amplified voices of a few roadies in fingerless mittens, paying out lengths of cabling and testing the mics. It was mid-afternoon when a man called Pod let me into the building and led me towards the dressing room, which at one point involved a little trespass across the corner of the stage. At the top of a flight of creaky wooden stairs he pointed towards a closed door with muffled voices and peculiar clicking sounds on the other side. Then he disappeared. I knocked on the door and it opened. A bespectacled David Gedge pushed his hand towards me and I shook it. Then I stepped across the threshold. Which I won't describe as like stepping into a parallel universe, but if I could have been in a band it would have been in a jangly, shambling band like the Wedding Present, and if I could have been a singer-songwriter I would have been a flat-vowelled northerner singing kitchen-sink, guitar-driven pop-rock, like David Gedge, and if I'd stuck at it for twenty years, like he has, I could have been playing Holmfirth Picturedrome tonight. In the fantasy, some other poet knocks on the door, and I open it.

What the fantasy didn't imagine was a full-size snooker table, which explains the clicking noises. Like Odysseus' bed, it looks like the building has been constructed around it and would have to be demolished if it is ever to be removed. Maybe the band and their small entourage were enjoying an orgy of sex and cocaine on the green baize and only picked up their cues when they heard me tapping at the door. I saw The Fall play here last week: does Mark E. Smith like a trip around the cloth before a gig? Did he incorporate the attendant paraphernalia, such as the triangle or a cube of blue chalk, into his post-concert tantrum? Did he kip on the table?

But other than this huge green oblong, the room is virtually empty, with a damp, clammy microclimate and an atmosphere of mild boredom. I don't suppose the Wedding Present are the kind of band who would be mobbed on the streets were they to set foot outside the building, or even be recognized for that matter, especially in Holmfirth on a weekend, when most people in the town are pensioners on bus trips from Swansea looking for Nora Batty's front door or Compo's grave. But here they must sit, as rock and roll dictates, waiting to make their entrance. I'm ushered towards the hospitality counter, which is less of a cornucopia of stimulation and indulgence and more like a stall at a county fair, or raffle prizes at a cricket club, consisting largely of sweeties, party snacks and a few bottles of mid-price wine, all presented in a neat little display. Maybe the hard stuff is behind the counter, though when the man himself chooses a glass of cranberry juice I decide to follow suit.

'Have you brought a tape recorder?'

'No, just these,' I say, holding up a notebook and pen.

He's thoughtful and softly spoken. I like him. We talk about Yorkshire even though he moved to Brighton at some stage, then we talk about Brighton even though he now lives in Los Angeles. I tell him that *Sea Monsters* is their best album, no question. And I tell him how politically important he is as a singer, even if it's just for singing in his own accent rather than some sort of transatlantic drawl, and why that bit on the *George Best* album, between 'Shatner' and 'Something and Nothing', when he's getting arsey with someone in the studio, talking about 'smoove distorted sounds' in a nasally Leeds accent, is so significant. He nods, then says, 'Actually, that wasn't me.' He's sitting on a firm plastic seat whereas I'm sinking into some flea-bitten old armchair, and to hear me he leans forward, with his arms folded across his chest and his legs crossed, so his toes are about level with my nose. And even though I'm not a fronter, I can now exclusively reveal that David Gedge wears what I would probably describe as sensible shoes.

SA: OK, shall we do the interview then?

DG: Haven't we started?

SA: Not yet. But it won't take long. Just a few questions.

DG: Fire away.

SA: David or Dave?

DG: David.

SA: Smoking or non-smoking?

DG: Non-smoking.

SA: Aisle or window?

DG: Er . . . aisle, if I'm going to America. Window coming here.

SA: *Magpie* or *Blue Peter*?

DG: *Blue Peter*.

SA: Purvis or Singleton?

DG: There's not much in it.

SA: Tea or coffee?

DG: Coffee.

SA: West Pier or Palace Pier?

DG: West Pier.

SA: Huddersfield or Halifax?

DG: Er . . . I don't really . . . er . . .

SA: The right answer's Huddersfield.

DG: Put me down for that, then.

SA: The Wedding Present or the Birthday Party?

DG: The Wedding Present.

SA: Hughes or Heaney?

DG: Hughes.

SA: Mick McManus or Kendo Nagasaki?

DG: Who are they?

SA: Wrestlers; 1970s.

DG: Pass.

SA: Wet shave or electric?

DG: Wet.

SA: Canine or feline?

DG: Canine.

SA: Batter or breadcrumbs?

DG: Batter.

SA: Celtic or Rangers?

DG: (mischievously): Rangers.

(Scottish voice from over by the snooker table: 'Fuck off.')

SA: Ketchup or HP?

DG: HP.

SA: *Pulp Fiction* or *Reservoir Dogs?*

DG: *Pulp Fiction.*

SA: Mum or Dad?

DG: You can't ask that.

SA: To be or not to be?

DG: To be.

SA: Marmite or Bovril?

DG: Marmite.

SA: Lennon or McCartney?

DG: No preference.

SA: Paul or Heather?

DG: Paul.

SA: *Swapshop* or *Tiswas?*

DG: *Tiswas.*

SA: Corduroy or denim?

DG: Corduroy.

SA: PC or Mac?

DG: PC.

SA: Brown or Blair?

DG: Blair.

SA: 'A God with a beard or a God without a beard?'

DG: Er . . . a God with a beard.

SA: Heaven or Las Vegas?

DG: Las Vegas.

SA: *Dandy* or *Beano?*

DG: *Beano.*

SA: *Revie* or *Reevie*?
DG: *Revie*.
SA: *Bough*-ie or *Bo*-ie?
DG: *Bo*-ie.
SA: Speak now or forever hold your peace?
DG: Speak now.
SA: The devil or the deep blue sea?
DG: The devil.
SA: Blur or Oasis?
DG: No preference.
SA: Scraps or bits?
DG: Scraps.
SA: Morrissey or Marr?
DG: Morrissey.
SA: All or nothing?
DG: All.
SA: Acoustic or electric?
DG: Electric.
SA: Last question: 'Should I Stay or Should I Go?'
DG: Er . . . you should stay. If you want to.
SA: No, I'll get out of your hair, I'm off to see the Wedding Present tonight. David Gedge, thanks very much.
DG: Pleasure.

All Things to All Men

♫

Yesterday lying alone in a bedroom,
Yesterday crying and dying of boredom,
But I was a showgirl, destined for stardom . . .

Today I'm the nurse getting off with the doctor
Tomorrow I'm shocked by a driving instructor

Today I'm the teacher who fancies the student
Tonight I'm the student who fancies the teacher
Tomorrow it's fun with a nun and a preacher

Today I'm the girl with a crush on her sister
Tonight I'm the traitor who teases the jailor
Tomorrow I'm taken down south by a sailor

Today I'm surprised by the size of the postman
Tonight I'm alone in the house with a truncheon
Tomorrow I'm frisked by a team of policemen

Today I'm the missus who calls for a plumber
Tonight I'm the stripper who swallows a python
Then bends over backwards to help out the juggler
Tomorrow I'm doused with a hose by a fireman

Gig

Today I'm a virgin at home on her lonesome
Who's joined by a soldier who makes it a twosome
Who's come with his brother who makes it a threesome
Who's come with his uncle who makes it a foursome
Then in walks a swordsman, an oarsman, a horseman
And dozens of pillaging Norsemen – it's awesome

The typist, the gymnast, the mistress, the matron
Yesterday lying alone in a bedroom
Yesterday crying and dying of boredom
But destined for stardom . . .

♫

Sung by Rebecca in the film *Pornography: the Musical*
(Century Films/Channel 4, 2003).

On the Road 11

Ottawa Writers' Festival, 20 April 2007. At the book signing:

Man: Didn't you read here two years ago?
Me: I did.
Man: Is that the same shirt?

The Best, the Worst, the First and the Last

STUDENTS UNION, MUSEUM ROAD
PORTENTS PRESENTS
Eyeless in Gaza and Felt
Ents. Hall Alex House
21st JANUARY 1984
8p.m. onwards   N°   **173**
Ticket   OVER 18s ONLY
£1.75p in advane £2 on the door
This ticket does not give Automatic Entry to P.P.S.U.

First gig I ever went to? The Skids, in the Great Hall at Huddersfield Poly; 1980, I think.

Best gig I ever went to? Eyeless in Gaza and Felt in the students union at Portsmouth Poly, 21 January 1984: £1.75 in advance, £2 on the door. Eight p.m. onwards. Not the greatest music ever made, or the greatest musicians, but my two favourite bands at the time, miraculously appearing on the same bill in the city where I just happened to be living. It was the language I was interested in as much as anything. Felt's first album went under the name of *Crumbling the Antiseptic Beauty* – I couldn't resist. And Eyeless in Gaza seemed preoccupied with nostalgia. A single, 'Kodak Ghosts Run Amok', was followed by the album *Photographs as Memories*. Their second album, *Caught in Flux*, was a beautifully packaged object, adorned with black-and-white snaps of boys on bikes and mothers in cardigans from days gone by. To someone like me, 250 miles from where I wanted to be and suffering from chronic homesickness, it was exactly the kind of introspective self-indulgence I'd been looking for. Plus I'd just read Aldous Huxley's book of the same name (the scene where someone chucks a dog out of an aeroplane is the only bit anyone ever remembers) so everything seemed to be pointing in the same direction. I wrote to Martyn Bates, one half of Eyeless in Gaza, asking him for the lyrics to the songs. I didn't have an address so I just posted it to Cherry Red Records in Orpington, Kent. A few weeks later he sent me a postcard of the Great Conqueror (his eyes coloured in with a pink highlighter pen) and the lyrics, all of them, in a neat but spiky hand, in printed rather than joined-up writing. I was obviously very impressionable at the time: I figured that if spiky, printed handwriting was good enough for Martyn Bates then it was good enough for me. Since that date, every character in every word I've ever penned has remained resolutely unconnected to the next. It's possible that I also considered becoming Symon Armytage, but I can find no documentary evidence to confirm it.

★

The worst gig I ever went to was Simply Red at Manchester's Nynex Arena. Free tickets, but that's no excuse. The band themselves were no worse than I thought they would be, although from where we were sitting Mick Hucknall looked like Charlie Drake, and people with no sense of rhythm shouldn't wear platform shoes. But it was the couple sitting next to us who really turned my stomach, a couple for whom every song was an 'our tune'. A few bars into every track, they'd share a knowing look and exchange a titter of excitement. The next moment they'd be standing on their seats, singing, snogging and swaying from side to side, not always in that order. Between numbers, she'd lift her hand towards his face, and he'd kiss the engagement ring. Every relationship is entitled to its musical highlights, and even though it wouldn't be my choice for a proposal soundtrack, there's no reason why a marriage underpinned by Simply Red should be any more or less stable than the next. But it was the undignified openness of it all that got to me in the end. The sheer absence of embarrassment. The complete lack of shame. That, and the image of a golden wedding fifty years hence, the anniversary waltz, a couple tottering to the dance floor to the strains of 'Holding Back the Years' or 'If You Don't Know Me by Now', illuminated by the quivering, naked flames from dozens of Zippo lighters. An image that haunts me to this day.

The worst poetry reading I ever went to was one of my own, in the small town of Strahan on the west coast of Tasmania. The venue was a kind of social club somewhere near the sea. There were six of us on the bill that night.

Of the five people in the 'audience', one was the organizer, one was Speedy Sue, and the other three had come to the club to play some sort of bingo game on a giant video screen. To stamp her authority on the evening and to ensure the attention of those people present, the organizer insisted the bingo machines be switched off, and reminded the punters they were in fact outnumbered by writers. Thus, in an atmosphere of growing resentment, the reading went ahead. I've always maintained that a poetry reading needs no more than a handful of listeners to be a meaningful and significant occasion, but I never thought I'd have to travel to the opposite side of the world to put this theory to the test. After the event, we went back to the off-season holiday cabins that were our lodgings to check for *Latrodectus hasselti* under the toilet seat. And the organizer set off into the Tasmanian night on her pushbike. She was wearing a safety helmet, attached to which was a little mirror on a stick, like the kind used by dentists to look for decaying teeth at the back of the mouth. It was a wing mirror, apparently, to check for overtaking cars, even though vehicles of any type seemed pretty thin on the ground. But I suppose if you've just subjected Tasmanian bingo players to an evening of Pommy literature against their will, you need to watch your back.

The best poetry reading I ever went to was also my first. Ted Hughes at Hebden Bridge Picture House: 1980? Same year as the Skids? When he parted the curtain, shuffled on stage and coughed into the microphone, I thought he was one of the backstage staff come to set up the lectern and perform a soundcheck. The cinema was full of students who were studying his poems at school. Everyone was trying to be cool and uninterested, but it's hard to feign nonchalance when you're being hypnotized. 'View of a Pig'. 'Bayonet Charge'. 'Hawk Roosting'. 'Pike'. Once I'd heard him I couldn't get the voice out of my head, and couldn't get the poems out of my system.

Ted Hughes left his mark wherever he went. You can still feel his presence in those towns and villages at the top end of the Calder Valley, which is peculiar in a way, because he wasn't much older than seven when he left the area. He made occasional return trips, but as far as the national census is concerned was never a permanent resident of that postcode again. Elmet, he called it, referring to the limits of an old Celtic kingdom, whose bolt-holes and smoke-holes took in the foothills of the lower Pennines and the steep-sided, wooded valleys of present-day West Riding. Members of the local community, he once said, were 'essentially a geological and meteorological phenomenon', as if they were all derived from rocks and rain. 'This helps to explain their obsessive concern through the ages with chills, bronchitis, pneumonia, rheumatism; with hot food and as much of it as can be had, and with wrapping up well.' It certainly tallies with my experience of West Yorkshire. More than half a century after Hughes left the area, a fair proportion of the conversation still revolves around homespun remedies for coughs and colds and typically takes place in a shop doorway while sheltering from the driving sleet. His description of the upper Calder as 'a naturally evolved local organism, like a giant protozoa' might seem at first like Hughesian hyperbole, but the implication – that the area exhibits a peculiar form of self-sufficiency – still feels very true, especially in the case of Hebden Bridge. Independence and isolation are two other words that come to mind when thinking of that town. Hughes once referred to Hebden Bridge as the cradle of the Industrial Revolution in textiles, the cradle of the Chartist movement, and even the cradle of the splitting of the atom. I'm not sure what he meant by that. He also dubbed it the hippie capital of Britain during the sixties, a status that persists, though the contemporary version of the hippie lifestyle is a slightly more compromised arrangement. Hebden Man could be stereotyped as a dreadlocked real-ale drinker, accompanied on his stroll along the towpath by a dog rescued from the local animal sanctuary. He sports a henna tattoo on his shoulder, wears clown trousers and a court jester hat. He juggles, plays the balalaika, and owns his own media production company in Manchester or Leeds. Hebden Woman, his life-partner, operates a henna tattoo parlour from the back of the wholefood cafe, runs yoga workshops and coordinates a website on out-of-body experiences. The legs of her baby, Fi-Fi Elderflower, dangle from a papoose slung from her neck. Hebden Bridge has also been described as the thinking person's Todmorden ('Tod' being a more working-class version of the same thing and the next stop on the train line) and is rumoured to be the home of a number of active covens, though one theory has it that the true occultism and kookiness has taken refuge in some of the darker nooks and crannies of the Calder Valley, such as Heptonstall or Luddenden.

Hughes once said, 'As a boy, all my more exciting notions gravitated upwards.' Standing outside number 1 Aspinall Street in Mytholmroyd, the house where he was born, it is not difficult to understand why. On one side of the valley stand the sentinels of blackened buildings and dark ridges. On the other looms Scout Rock, the blank quarry face that blots out all but the highest movements of the sun. Along the corridor of the valley, traffic rumbles through at a rate that has only increased through the years, despite the opening of the M62. In these circumstances, the valley becomes a kind of trap, a narrow funnel of darkness and fumes. In his memory, and with the poet cranking up the rhetoric, it then becomes a gorge, a ditch, a trough, a pit, and ultimately (and perhaps inevitably) a trench. It is a place to be avoided or escaped and the only escape route is up. A couple of years ago, seeing me mooching around, the occupant of number 3 Aspinall Street invited me up to peer out of her skylight, just as Hughes might have peered out of the attic next door. There was almost an audible change in air pressure as she pushed open the Velux window. I poked my head through the hatch, and looked out on to a hawk's-eye world of rooftops, moorland and sky.

Full Moon

It's midnight in Luddenden,
midnight in Luddenden,
midnight in Luddenwhen
all of a suddenden
here comes a shape in a cloak and a hood.
They're holding hands in Luddendenfoot
and there's trouble in Luddenden,
trouble in Luddenden,
Luddenden, Luddenden, Luddendenfoot.

Luddendenfoot, Luddendenfoot,
they're forming a circle in Luddendenfoot,
but the frumpy librarian's really a witch
who's bedding a druid from Hebenden Bridge —
hubble and bubble there's trouble in Luddenden
trouble in Luddenden,
Luddenden, Luddenden, Luddendenfoot.

Luddendenfoot, Luddendenfoot,
they're closing rank in Luddendenfoot.
Round the back of a hut
a goat gets killed with a woodenden clubenden,
chickens are slaughtered,
Catholics are neutered,
the queen of the covenden

working up phlegm with soya milk bubblegum
gobs on the graves of the great and the goodenden,
curses the vicars
of Mixenden, Illingworth, Warley and Ovenden.
Look, Mother, look,
in the locked-up, blacked-out community centre
they're burning a book. Nothing is sacred —
they're writhing and shaking, they're stark-bollock naked
they're painting their genitals green and magenta,
they're veggies as well but they're eating placenta
they're all in a huddleden
daubing themselves with henna and mudenden,
here comes the knife and here comes the bloodenden.
Call for the cops —
there's trouble in Luddenden,
trouble in Luddenden,
trouble tonight and it's double in Luddenden,
Luddenden, Luddenden, Luddenden, Luddenden,
Luddenden, Luddenden, Luddenden, Luddenden,
Luddenden, Luddenden, Luddendenfoot.

Young Marble Giants
Clyro Court
26 May 2007

Details are correct at time of going to press. We reserve the right to change these times and information available if you dictate. Tickets cannot be accepted for refund or resale. **Note:** The management reserve to contact the Box Office if any reason concerning this ticket

Event Name Young Marble Giants

Hay Festival
of Literature
and The
Arts Ltd

Venue*: Clyro Court

Time*: 20:00

Customer Reference DoorA4HR35AD

Sale Date/Time 26/05/2007 15:21:29

Ticket No: 69765

Event No: 122

Ticket Type: Complimentary

Ticket Cost £ 0.00

Customer: A Doorsale4

VAT Reg. No. 826 3209 39
www.hayfestival.com

(* Times or Venues may occasionally have to be changed after tickets are issued)

Advice to poets: beware the 'gala reading'. There are two types. Type I is the more common strain, and is easily diagnosed even when camouflaged as a 'celebration'. A mopping-up exercise, basically, it brings together all the poets who during the course of a week have been running workshops, giving lectures or speaking on panels, and sweeps them into a single event in an oversized venue on the last night of a literary festival. The reading begins in a spirit of triumph and optimism, with an opening address on the power of words and the VITALITY AND VARIETY of the contemporary poetry scene (after which the organizer and his team leave the venue by a side exit to enjoy a cabaret and free bar in the festival club). For the next four hours there is a slow but marked fall in atmospheric pressure, as an indeterminate and increasing number of performers line up to take the stage, including spouses, sponsors, novelists and members of the audience who have HEEDED THE CALL OF VERSE. With sunlight breaking in the east and to the accompaniment of the dawn chorus, the final poet on the bill reads to an audience consisting entirely of close relatives or personal carers. The only other person present is the caretaker, grinding his teeth and jangling a fob of keys.

The type II gala reading is a much more tightly controlled affair, beginning with a briefing session in the green room where poets are issued with strict instructions. The reading will begin at 7.31 and end at 8.29 precisely so the venue can be made ready for the next event: an interview with an environmental activist who escaped his guerrilla captors in the Peruvian jungle, or a reading by a Lincolnshire housewife facing a life-threatening illness without medical intervention whose daily blog created a BIDDING FRENZY amongst agents and editors and whose book is set to become a PUBLISHING SENSATION. In other words, someone who REALLY HAS SUFFERED, for whom the organizers are expecting QUITE A CROWD. Poets will read for no more than three minutes and fifteen seconds each, will remain on stage at all times in a preordained seating plan, and will appear in alphabetical order ('So you'll kick us off, Simon, OK?'), although the first couple of poems will almost certainly be lost beneath the noise of shuffling latecomers and microphone feedback. Valuing alacrity over accuracy, the host will rattle through his introductory notes at a bewildering speed, so even in the unlikely event of their names being correctly pronounced, poets will find themselves being born and brought up in cities they have never visited, being the authors of books that sound like cruel parodies of their own, and being the well-deserved winners of prizes actually awarded to their bitterest rivals. As the event progresses, the host's sense of emergency is transmitted to the poets, more so with the brave hostage or frail blogger now visible in the wings, because it would be inhuman to steal even a few minutes from a person who for the past five years has been manacled to a banana tree, or someone for whom TIME IS RUNNING OUT. In these circumstances, the type II gala reading becomes the literary equivalent of the Grand National: a mad, undignified scramble towards the finishing post, with fallers at the first, a multiple pile-up at Canal Turn and several poets crossing the line like riderless horses, minus their composure and self-respect.

The type II gala has the advantage of being QUICKLY OVER compared to the type I, which has the inertia and ennui of a televised House of Lords debate. At a type I in Sweden in 1996 I read at midday, then retired to the hotel and watched the whole of the Liverpool–United FA Cup Final (Cantona, 1–0) before strolling back to the venue in the early evening to do an encore. On the other hand the type II, with its emphasis on punctuality and continual attendance, tends to restrict liberty and limit movement. Making it impossible, for example, to slip off for an hour or so to see a band. Making it impossible to go and hear Cardiff's legendary Young Marble Giants, for example, performing in a country house just a couple of miles away. Making it simply OUT OF THE QUESTION, even if you missed them the first time around, even if this is a once-only-never-to-be-repeated reunion gig, and even if the night in question is your birthday.

Goodbye to All That

I don't do eBay. For the person who works from home, there are enough daily distractions and displacement activities available on the internet without becoming embroiled in a global electronic auction. Also, when we were house-hunting a few years ago, we visited the property of a self-confessed eBay addict, and I've never been able to dislodge the memory. By her own admission she spent the greater portion of her waking life in a dimly lit study, bidding for unwanted items and, judging by the amount of tat and trammel cluttering her home, usually winning them. The front door wouldn't fully open because of the table football wedged behind it. In the alcove under the stairs stood a full-size jukebox. Every shelf sagged with the weight of toby jugs and commemorative tableware, and Beanie Babies of every zoomorphic shape and size perched shoulder to shoulder along bookshelves and curtain rails. The whole place was an emporium of utter crap. She was a buyer, not a seller. Maybe when she was younger she'd spent hours flicking through her mother's Grattan catalogue, fantasizing about owning the lot. And if the World Wide Web hadn't evolved in her lifetime, she might have become one of those eccentric but harmless spinsters who owns about twenty cats and leaves her modest savings to a church roof appeal or a seal sanctuary. But along came the internet, and up popped eBay, the great cosmic jumble sale, in which a whale's penis or a fragment of moon rock can be yours with just the touch of a button and in the blink of an eye. Even as we left, a UPS truck was pulling up outside, and two delivery men in their brown and yellow uniforms were unloading another consignment, including a stag's head mounted on a toilet seat and a stuffed otter in a standing position with a patch over one eye and a cutlass swinging from its belt.

So I don't do eBay, but Speedy Sue does. She has a nose for a bargain and a knack of getting what she wants. Her first purchase was a pair of neon-pink Barbie Rollerblades for the Tudge's fourth birthday. They were about thirty quid cheaper than in the shops and were being sold from an address about twenty miles away, which meant we could collect them ourselves and save on the postage. In a part of Wakefield I didn't even know existed I drove through a sprawling housing estate whose only distinguishing feature seemed to be a grassed play area with a pylon in the middle of it. The house we were looking for was shrouded on three sides by an overgrown hedge and had a picture of a deranged-looking Alsatian dog in the window subtitled with the words 'I LIVE HERE'. The door opened on the chain, and after we'd passed the money through the gap, out came the goods, fully packaged and with the security tab still intact. For a few naïve moments, I considered the tragic story behind these gaudy Rollerblades – the story of a life unlived, of presents bought but never given, and a small grave in a nearby churchyard with a teddy bear tied to a wreath and a nursery rhyme carved on the gravestone. But in the murky hallway beyond, there was just enough light and just enough time to see dozens of other boxes of 'as-new' Barbie Rollerblades stacked against the wall and up the stairs. When I was a probation officer, this kind of commerce usually took place in a locked pub on a Sunday afternoon. We drive home with mixed emotions, quietly glad that the goods in question aren't second-hand and haven't been sullied by the smelly feet of another child, but slightly concerned that the gift we are giving to the love of our life is, in all likelihood, hot.

A second eBay transaction a few months later had a similar atmosphere of subterfuge and deceit, even though we were the vendors this time and the item we were flogging was 100 per cent legit. At an equidistant point and at a prearranged time in the late evening, we rendez-vous with a couple from Wrexham on a slip road of the M56. Unchecked, the foldaway pram was transferred from one vehicle to another, and a wad of used fivers, uncounted, changed hands. The woman sitting in the other car was pregnant. The man doing the deal was silent. So were we. Then, without a handshake or even a cheerio, they went their way – towards Mid Wales and parenthood – and we went ours. I'm remembering all this as I log on to eBay to see that the bidding on a really wonderful electric guitar has reached the £200 mark. Like I said, I don't do eBay but Speedy Sue does, and the account I'm monitoring is hers, and the electric guitar she is selling – at the request of her husband – is mine.

The great thing about an electric guitar is this: it makes you sound like you can play. Acoustic guitars exaggerate all your inadequacies, especially guitars with tight, cheese-wire strings, which make you sound like you're wearing boxing gloves. With an electric guitar, all you need to do is crank the gain knob up to the top and you're Jimi Hendrix. The bad thing about an electric guitar is that it reminds you of everything you're not. It leans against the wall, as cool as you like, while you watch TV, read books and get older. The most obvious symbol of ambition and attitude on the day it enters your life, over time it becomes a metaphor for all the songs you'll never write and the gigs you'll never play. So it has to go. I'll keep the acoustic Yamaha for the odd strum here and there, and Speedy Sue has her Ovation, from her Speedy Bears days, just in case. But the Stratocaster, the Fender Stratocaster, the guitar that makes me a legend in my own living room . . . it has to go.

It's a Jap Strat, apparently. I didn't especially know this, but my friend Alan, a guitar addict, has given it the once-over and found some serial number on the back and now knows its entire pedigree. He writes the blurb and Speedy Sue takes a photograph. All I do is watch the auction, which finally tops out at just less than 300 quid. The moment the hammer goes down the guitar becomes the legal property of someone called Sean residing in County Clare. And my life as a rock star – no matter how non-existent – is officially at an end.

Ever try wrapping a guitar? Feels like you're wrapping a person. A person of peculiar shape, admittedly, with a small knobbly head, a long thin neck and no legs. But a person all right. When you roll him on to his back his heartstrings twang. Then each muffled plea becomes fainter and more pitiful with every layer of paper, and every round of gaffer tape binds him tighter and tighter, until he is mummified into silence once and for all. For good measure, I then slide him into the body bag of a black plastic refuse sack and take him outside. Under the shelter of the porch I leave him to be collected by FedEx. For two, three and then four days he's still there, to the point where I'm wondering if it wouldn't have been kinder just to slip him into the canal one evening, put him out of his misery. But on day five, when I get home, he's gone.

I go into the house, make a cup of tea, and listen to Shostakovich.

On the Road 12

Latitude Festival in Suffolk. I judge this to be the most rock-and-roll event I've ever done, not just because I'm on the same bill as the Magic Numbers, Midlake and the Good, the Bad and the Queen, but because I've been given a performer's wristband. I'm reading just after lunch in the Stand Up Poetry Tent, and wonder if it will constitute a breach of contract if I sit down. I start by introducing a poem called 'The Stuff'.

> Me: I used to work in Manchester . . .
> One Person: Hurray!
> Me: . . . with drug users.
> Several People: HURRAY!

Nodding Dog

♪

So it all went to pot, girl,
when you talked to the shop-girl,
about white Rolls-Royces and mobile disco vans.

And you opened a page, girl,
full of pageboys and cakes, girl,
and honeymoon retreats and wedding dress meringues.

Chorus:
So let the disco play
Del Shannon's 'Runaway',
then picture us two looking naff
inside a wine-glass photograph.
Someday soon we'll live as one
but something tells you something's wrong,
I'm a nodding dog but God I'm not fooling anyone.

So your mother's cut up, girl,
so your dad beats me up, girl,
and your brother's playing clackers with my knackers and
my knees.

Gig

Now you want all your records back,
and your books and your Apple Mac,
and the Love Heart we licked when we were just sixteen.

(Chorus)

Sod the sarnies and seating plan,
sod the aunties and vol-au-vents,
sod the strangers queuing up to shake my hand.

Let's just hit Las Vegas, girl,
in T-shirts and trainers, girl,
and we'll walk the aisle in that dumb and distant land.

So let the disco play
Del Shannon's 'Runaway',
then picture us two looking naff
inside a wine-glass photograph.
Someday soon we'll live as one
but something tells you something's wrong,
I'm a nodding dog but God I'm not fooling anyone.

♫

The Scaremongers

The Scaremongers

. . . and I listen to Shostakovich. Except the Boy Smith phones up a couple of weeks later and says something like, 'Why didn't we ever get that band together when we had the chance?' And I say something like, 'Don't know. A shame, really.' And he says, 'Yeah. Well, why don't we do it now?' And because I can't think of a logical response to his question (there are dozens of logical responses to his question, I just can't think of one immediately) I say, 'OK, let's do it.' And by the time I put the phone down, I am the singer-songwriter of a two-man band; one being a perfectly respectable web manager who wears glasses to read, the other being a forty-four-year-old poet and father. Two hours later, having sobered up, I call him back and hint at some of the obstacles that would appear to stand between our new band and rock-and-roll megastardom. Like the fact that we live 223 miles apart. But Craig (for that is his name) has an answer to every possible problem, and because I am already smitten by his fantasy, I am inclined to believe every word he says.

In truth, he makes some valid points. Twenty years ago, he recalls, we sat in a ground-floor bedsit in East Didsbury in front of a three-bar fire with a duvet over our shoulders (separate duvets, that is) and a plate of toast between us, trying to write songs on a battered old guitar and record them on a battered old cassette player. We

Gig

were two students from mild-mannered villages in West Yorkshire; I was a trainee probation officer and he was a trainee librarian – not exactly ideal material for the first chapter of a rock autobiography. Back then, to make any progress would have meant putting together a decent demo tape, getting signed to a label and releasing a record. But we had no money, no instruments worth owning, no contacts and no particular talent. Given that all the bands we admired the most had overcome all those difficulties and more, it's possible to speculate that we had no desire either. From where we stood, it was like staring at the north face of Everest with nothing more than a stepladder and a ball of string.

To a certain extent, the same was true of poetry. In Huddersfield in the mid-eighties, there was one very modest bookshop with an even more modest poetry section. I'd read or bought all their poetry books in a single summer, and ordering more was time-consuming and pricey. The public library had its own eccentric and eclectic collection, but never the collections I wanted to read, and quite frankly it was quicker to *publish* a volume of poems than fill out an inter-library loan form and wait for the books to arrive. Beyond that, it was either a case of blagging entry into the polytechnic library (where books could be read but not borrowed) or making an expensive trip to Leeds or Manchester. These days it's hard to imagine life without complete and instant access to everything. Some of my younger students at Manchester Met have grown up with the idea that if it doesn't appear in the first ten entries of Google, it doesn't exist. The internet is where they get their information and how they share their ideas. Craig Smith Theory says it's also where they get their music. And accordingly, it's where they're going to get ours.

The most important decision for any band to make is its name. It defines the whole direction of the project. Maybe to the outsider it doesn't matter at all, otherwise how would bands with dumb names like Bat For Lashes or Steely Dan or Clap Your Hands Say Yeah or even U2 have done so well? But to the band itself the name is EVERYTHING. And you would be forgiven for thinking that with the whole of the dictionary to choose from, finding the right name would be a straightforward task. But almost every word or combination of words carries unwanted luggage. It's too indie-pop (The Wheelybins) or it's too derivative (Dragnet). Or it's too eighties (The Cagoules), too easily mispronounced (The Xoanons), too easily misunderstood (What's New on the High Street?), too self-conscious (The Autodidacts), too self-deprecating (the Has-Beens), too disingenuously self-deprecating (The Late Lamented), too seventies (Trespass), too heavy (Troopcarrier), too nineties (the Jupiter and Barnsley Choral Society), too daft (Kneetrembler), too capricious (Fond), too northern (Pork Pie), too camp (The Shame-faced Sparrows), too much like the sound of a real ale or a brand of rolling tobacco (Hobson's Choice), too playground (The Wagon Wheels), too cheesy (Terry and June), too hostage-to-fortune (Royal and Ancient, i.e. which one are you, then?) etc. We're absolutely determined not to choose anything too literary or anything that makes promises we can't live up to, hence Jude the

Obscure and Pepperspray are vetoed at an early stage. Every time we *do* find what we think is a decent name, it turns out that it already belongs to a neo-punk band from Ohio who, even if they haven't released any records as yet, have a swanky website, have patented the brand, registered their trademark and own the domain name. Part of me thinks that we should say sod it, do our own thing, go our own way, and if the universe wants us it can come and find us. But Craig Smith Theory says otherwise, and it speaks the truth. Arctic Monkeys might not be the best band name ever, but the incongruous coupling of those two words ensures that any half-decent search engine will pinpoint the required target within a fraction of a second. Call yourself Fishfingers, on the other hand, and by the time would-be listeners have waded through details of Tesco's latest frozen food offers or the innumerable web pages dedicated to the seafaring and decidedly dubious grey-bearded loon Captain Birdseye, they will have abandoned the search. After two weeks of giddy emailing and misspelt text-messaging, we narrow it down to a mere 280, from which we agree on a final shortlist:

Peroxide Miracles
Tracksuit Jesus
The Numpties
The Artisans
Sheriffs of Play-Doh
The Awkward Squad
The Fire Brigade
Uncle Bob

Katnip
Nosebag
Brantub
Left Hand Down
The Lemsip Junkies
I Wish I Was You
I Wish You Were Me
The Carpet Fitters
The Rookery
The Soft White Pillowcase Boys
Two-Man Kayak
Disgrace
Zirconium
Thatcher Versus Thatcher
Treehouse
The Snoods
Broom Cupboard
Dirty Brenda
The Foot Soldiers
Donkeywork
The Lifetime
The George
Tuesday Thursday
Liquorice Crowbar
The Mules
The Robinsons
Air Sea Rescue
Jiggerfish
The Bearcatchers
The Naked and the Dead
The Nerve

The Absolute Nerve
The Shameless Helligans
The Lunar Landscape
The Gone
The Gone But Not Forgottens
The Gone and Good Riddance
Death's Door
Shanks's Pony
Taliban Hairdo
Intellectual Shambles
Pseudo-Tribal Self-Aggrandizement
The Loss Leaders
White Rastas Are Patronizing
The White Rastas
The Patrons
Phoney Baloney Patois Hoax
The Anti-Mariah Careys
So Many Band Names (So Little Time)
The Make-Dos
The Tarquins
Blood Orange
Myopia
Bradford Park Avenue
Paso Doble
Dragonfly
Stair-rods
The Singing Electricians
Dibner
Meltham is a Dangerous Place
Direct Current
The Calendar Girls

Bandit
The Even Stevens
Saliva
Private Doberman
!
?
@
The Terriers
The Western Terrace
Sparklines
Future Purchasing Power
And/Or
The Gateway to Perfect Pop
Leper Colony
Tactile
Wainwright
Arkwright
Arclight
Klieglight
Wheelwright
Millwright
Schofield
The Apartment
New York Loft Living (Comes to Marsden)
Brahma!
The Book of Bokonon
Dormobile
The Stories
The Storeys
Kids These Days Know Nowt!
The Bejesus

The Graze
Gauze
The Cells
Hoss

In the end (and we're not sure how) we become The Scaremongers. When I say to people, 'We've decided on a band name,' and they say, 'Oh yeah, what is it?' and I say, 'The Scaremongers,' they say, 'Yeah, that works,' or they nod appreciatively. Which is a good sign. It also satisfies my desire for a definite article, contains a nodding reference to our beloved Orange Juice, and is appropriate to the project in the sense that at this stage we are little more than an alarmist rumour. Having said that, we have already gathered quite an entourage, including a bass player, a lead guitarist, a harmonica-player-cum-video-director, a Bez (my mate Slug, the world's coolest dancer), a critic (my mate Slug, who has cast an eye across the proposed lyrics for one song and decided that 'bed' and 'shed' are rubbish rhymes), a distributor (my mate Tony at Vinyl Tap), a merchandiser (my mate Rick: 'I'll flog yer T-shirts for yer'), a photographer (Slug again, in a pub in Streatham one night with a camera) and an in-house artist, along with a label name: Corporation Pop. Genius, except that no one outside West Yorkshire seems to know that Corporation Pop is a euphemism for water. We have not played a single note in anger, yet we are already in danger of becoming 'a collective'. We've also been the topic of a Radio 2 phone-in, or rather I invited listeners on the *Mark Radcliffe Show* to text in with suggestions for names. The only one I can remember is Fantastic Gammon. My dad, via the show, has also got wind of the proposed band.

'Thought of a name yet? How about Midlife Crisis?'

For a moment, I'm almost tempted.

Here's how the whole thing will work. Craig will write the music. From his studio (i.e. back bedroom) he will also sequence the percussion, record guide tracks for bass and lead guitar, download and mix in the Continental organ, orchestrate the composition, set up a website, oversee the design of an image, upload photographs and text, conscript session musicians, liaise with the studio, drive up to Huddersfield to practise, devise a business strategy, provide instruments, and take care of all the other unforeseen issues that undoubtedly lie ahead of us. For my part, I will sing the songs. As a division of labour it might appear unfair, but as an acknowledgement of our particular talents, it is completely appropriate. I will also, being a writer, write the lyrics, though when the songs arrive, it's no surprise that some of his dummy or 'sacrificial' lyrics are good enough to keep. I think of Craig as a school friend, though we actually met at the now legendary (as far as we're concerned) poetry-writing workshops at Huddersfield Poly, so he's no mug with the alphabet, and his last book of poems, *A Quick Word with a Rock and Roll Late Starter*, seems suddenly prophetic. Most things in Huddersfield have been demolished and redeveloped since we first met, most things that is apart from the Merrie England coffee houses where we sat and wrote poems together. Not exactly City Lights bookshop, but the only place in town where we could scribble and talk and stay warm without being moved on or having to spend money. Occasionally one of the Merrie Maids, in their scarlet aprons, would lift up our books or papers and wipe down the table with a damp cloth, but other than that we were left alone. The last time I counted there were five Merrie Englands in Huddersfield. Five olde worlde coffee shoppes, including a drive-through! The franchise has also proliferated into Halifax. It's interesting to think that while many of the town's landmarks have disappeared, including the old football ground and several cinemas, these completely synthetic and fabricated institutions have stayed the course.

I don't pretend to understand how Craig builds up the songs on his laptop. Actually, that's a lie: I do pretend to understand. When he tells me what he's going to do and how he's going to do it, I reply with, 'Yes, that's probably a good idea,' or I say, 'I think that's exactly what needs to happen.' After a few weeks we have a couple of tunes taking shape, and it's my turn to start on the lyrics. The first drafts are way too convoluted, more like bad poems than anything else. If writing poems is like building up a papier-mâché or matchstick model, layer by careful layer, piece by precarious piece, then the process of lyric writing, for me anyway, is more like whittling a piece of wood, stripping and slicing away until something clear and smooth comes into view. We're thinking, in old-fashioned terms, of a double-A-side. One song, 'Nodding Dog', will tell the story of a reluctant bridegroom. The other, 'You Can Do Nothing Wrong (In My Eyes)', is almost a love song. Two people list each other's faults before confessing their unconditional, eternal and involuntary devotion to each other. It's revved-up pop, driven on by an irresistible dance rhythm and floating harmonies. It's also a duet, with one part for a man and another for a female voice.

Craig: 'Do you know anyone who can sing?'
Me: 'Not really. Oh, wait a minute.'

Speedy Sue is in the garden repotting a begonia when I make the suggestion, and she hesitates for at least one millisecond before saying yes. She is, in the parlance, most definitely UP FOR IT. A few evenings later, with the Tudge in bed and a few drinks inside us, we decide to give it a go. On top of the false Victorian fireplace the iPod pumps out the laptop-assembled, instrumental version of 'You Can Do Nothing Wrong (In My Eyes)'. And face to face, with one hand each on a trembling lyric sheet, we sing.

Did you ever sing in front of your loved one? It's a little bit like undressing together for the first time. Perfectly appropriate of course, and completely acceptable, not to mention absolutely necessary. But a little bit embarrassing, nevertheless, and executed with a certain degree of awkwardness. We've been together now for umpteen years, but apart from the odd nursery rhyme sung in unison at the request of the Tudge, I don't believe we have ever exposed the nakedness of our voices to each other. To extend the nudity metaphor, though, the self-consciousness only lasts for the first couple of run-throughs, after which it all becomes quite exciting. A little bit fruity, even? Is this why John couldn't resist making Yoko an honorary Beatle, or the reason why Paul offered Linda a tambourine? Is the hormonal frisson generated by vocal harmonics the explanation to the musical conundrum that was Peters and Lee? After an hour or so, I don't even care what the neighbours might think if they hear, or if they see. We are Mr and Mrs Armitage, singing to each other in the middle of the living room in the early evening, and we haven't even drawn the curtains.

Are The Scaremongers the only band ever to take a packed lunch into the studio? Craig stays over the night before, and in the morning we're up early buttering bread and choosing items from the fruit bowl. It's not just because we're thinking of our stomachs; hiring a recording studio isn't cheap, even in Huddersfield, and with the meter running all the time we don't want to be standing in a sandwich shop for half an hour waiting for a bacon buttie. Before we go, and for reasons I can't quite explain, I do two things that are completely out of character: I apply moisturizing cream, and I wear a hat. Then we set off, not exactly an entourage of coolness and credibility (me in a family saloon with a booster seat in the back, Craig in a rented Nissan Micra) but a cameo of excitement and anticipation.

The studio is a single-storey, brick-built, windowless building on the edge of a trading estate, just inside the ring road. It also borders Huddersfield's red-light area, which means the surrounding pavements are littered with the discarded wrappings of sex and the discharged instruments of heroin abuse. Inside, the dark and airless building is divided into three sections. The central part is the largest, the 'cubicle', housing all the computers, all the screens, all the desks and all the consoles with all their sliders, knobs and buttons. Through the glass, at the far end, is the recording studio itself, including a separate voice-booth, inside which stands an enormous microphone. To the unconfident singer, this mean-looking device appears capable of magnifying every vocal imperfection and amplifying it a hundredfold. Nearest to the entrance, the reception area contains a small bathroom, a small kitchenette (including a kettle that makes the water glow red when it's on and blue when it's off) and a comfy settee. On the wall are framed photographs of other bands, most of them local, who have recorded here, including a colour picture of Embrace. Embrace are Huddersfield's only true rock-and-roll success story (or Bradford's, or Halifax's, depending on where you position the small West Yorkshire town of Bailiff Bridge, and whether you want to claim Embrace as your own or deny any association with them). Even Noel Gallagher couldn't derail their journey towards the upper reaches of the album charts. At a time when every syllable that came out of the Oasis camp was front-page news, he was asked to comment on the up-and-coming, bubbling-under, tipped-for-the-top, next-big-thing Embrace. Fixing lead singer Danny McNamara in his sights, he is reported to have replied, 'That cunt wants singing lessons.' Despite which, they made it. Sort of. I once sat next to Embrace on a late train from London back to Leeds. Standard class. I didn't recognize them until Newark Northgate, but they had a kind of sheen about them which set them apart from other travellers. It would have been nice to chat with them and to have paid them a few genuine compliments, but the phrase 'Excuse me, are you Embrace?' seemed grammatically imprecise, and in the hour that followed I couldn't decide on the correct syntactical for-mulation to open the conversation. On another occasion, when I guest-edited a northern edition of the *Big Issue*, I wrote to them asking if they would give an interview. They replied (or more probably their *people* replied) that they would, but only if they could have the front cover. Maybe Embrace (or more probably their *people*) see Embrace as a pin-up band. But for a magazine conceived to help the homeless (i.e. people with nowhere to pin things) I determined their response to be perfectly tasteless.

Jason, the studio engineer, doesn't know if we are two middle-aged men with more imagination than sense trying to live out the rock-and-roll daydream of our youth (we are) or two guys trying to make a really good record (we are), and without ever addressing the issue directly we reach a kind of negotiated settlement in which our ambitions and our limitations might be comfortably accommodated. Craig impresses Jason with his know-ledge of early synthesizers and computerized recording systems (yawn), while I excel at coffee-making operations with the space-age kettle. Craig's bass-playing brother Glen lends a bit of glamour to the project by turning up in a big Jag, accompanied by lead-guitar-playing Geoff 'Birdman' Bird whose grungy, chin-length, straw-coloured hair is a welcome contrast to our regulation crops and our flecks of grey.

Being in a recording studio is boring. Especially if you're the singer. Hours pass and barely a note is struck. Whole days slide by with nothing to listen to except strings being tuned and amps being tweaked and guitar licks being repeated over and over and over and over again. Then suddenly, and without any particular warning or special preparation, you're ushered into the glass closet, the door is closed behind you, a green light flashes and YOU'RE ON. Speedy Sue pops up to sing her bit; she's done it before, so she's in and out in no time. Like someone nipping in and out of the changing room in Monsoon during her lunch break to try on a dress. I, on the other hand, am not so quick. Maybe it's the headphones I'm having to wear; under normal circumstances I can hear what comes out of my mouth because the sound of my voice travels directly into my ear. But this is like being partially deaf, trying to work out not only how loud I'm singing but what key I'm singing in by the vibration of the bones in my cheeks and jaw. Or maybe I'm just useless. My first take is terrible. My second take is worse. My third take is timid. My fourth take is met with silence from the cubicle. Through the glass I can see them all talking but I can't tell what they're saying. 'OK, ready to try again?' Craig asks me, after a few minutes. Eventually I get the thumbs-up, and am allowed to leave the aquarium and return to the mixing desk. When I hear the playback, I immediately blush. They say that when you hear a recording of your own singing it's uncomfortable, because it sounds like somebody else. But this is uncomfortable for a different reason: because it sounds like me.

At the end of two days of cutting and pasting, compressing and extending, turning things up or down and fading things in and out, we take a CD of the two songs into the reception area and flop out on the comfy settee and play it back on the cheap hi-fi. The inference being that this is what it will sound like to OUR FANS. Then we troop back into the cubicle, and after a few more minutes of flickering lights and whirring motors, the trays of a dozen CD-burners spontaneously open, ejecting twelve shiny discs. These are ours. To keep. To do with what we will. We pay up – in cash. Then after a few words in the car park, and avoiding the enticements of the call girls across the road and the attention of a patrolling police vehicle, Craig heads back down the M1 in his diddy-car, and I drive out into upstate Huddersfield with the stereo system playing louder than I ever knew it could play.

It's a great record. Obviously. OK, it isn't great, but it is good. Well, I'm kind of biased, but the same people who thought The Scaremongers was a good name think that 'You Can Do Nothing Wrong (In My Eyes)' c/w 'Nodding Dog' is a good record. And if it was rubbish, they'd say so. Wouldn't they? They're not sycophants. They're not The Sycophants to our The Scaremongers, are they? What people think matters to us – like everybody on the planet we'd rather be loved than despised and, given the choice, would prefer not to be thought of as a pair of idiots. But in the end, it's about different and better things. One: friendship. Two: getting off our backsides and doing something instead of just blabbing about it. Three: being in a band and making a record – we can die happy now. Four: one minute past midnight on New Year's Eve in a farmhouse on the Yorkshire moors, when the swirling, dizzying sound of 'You Can Do Nothing Wrong (In My Eyes)' sweeps the whole party into the whirlpool of the dance floor. And five: driving home from a reading one night, playing Beat the iPod, when the first few bars of 'Nodding Dog' erupt through the speakers. Saying to myself, I know who this is. This is The Scaremongers. This is Us.

We're going to print a few hundred CDs, give them away, maybe sell a few. We're going to record about a dozen songs, and put them all on one disc, and call it an album. Apart from that, we're not sure. In true Spinal Tap style, Craig orders a T-shirt with The Scaremongers' logo on it, but gets the dimensions wrong. It is, to all intents and purposes, a white T-shirt with a postage stamp on the chest. The same happens with the business card, which comes back from the printers exactly half the size of a regular business card with the words 'The Scaremongers' amputated from the waist down.

'It's kind of enigmatic,' says Slug, our new self-appointed manager and image guru, at least for this evening. It's Craig's birthday and we're sitting in his kitchen drinking a bottle of sparkling wine from coffee-stained mugs. 'By the way, that rhyme: dead and shed. It's rubbish.'

If we do ever get round to recording a full album, I want to call it *And Charlie Got Something He Likes Too*. Craig doesn't. Are we about to split up already? In the same conversation, the subject of 'playing live' rears its ugly head. I say that we need to think about it very carefully, that we would need months of rehearsal, that it isn't something we should rush into, and that there could be nothing worse than standing on stage in front of a live audience sounding like a prat, looking like a plank and feeling like a prick. But the prevailing opinion emanating from the other corners of the table is this: that it doesn't matter if you've made one single or a dozen platinum-selling albums, because until you've played live, you haven't even come close. In other words, you're not really a band at all until after your first gig.

*

A month or so later I'm on the internet searching for Woods' music shop. If you live in Huddersfield and you want an instrument, you go to Woods'. That's how it works. Everyone knows that. Pianos. Drums. Piccolos. Sheet music. A tray of overpriced records in plastic sleeves, including *Tubular Bells*. Plectrums, flageolets and kazoos in the glass cabinet. Guitars hanging up on the wall. The bloke with the limp. But the World Wide Web hasn't heard of Woods'. Neither has the phone book, or the Yellow Pages, or 118118. In the end I phone the only person I can think of who knows everything there is to know about Huddersfield.

> Me: Where's Woods'?
> Mum: Where's what?
> Me: Where's Woods'?
> Mum: What's Woods'?
> Me: Woods' shop.
> Mum: Woods' what?
> Me: Woods' shop.
> Mum: Woods' music shop?
> Me: Yes.
> Mum: What about it?
> Me: Where is it?

Mum: It's closed down. Or it got taken over.
Me: Woods'? When?
Mum: Years ago. Why?
Me: I need to buy an electric guitar.

There's long, considered pause, then she says, 'No. It's gone. You're too late.'

You Can Do Nothing Wrong
(In My Eyes)

♪

BOY

Like all the rest, you weep at sunsets in the west.

GIRL

Like all the least, you sleep through sunrise in the east.

BOY

You're a daddy's girl, he buys you dresses and you twirl.

GIRL

You're mummy's boy, in snake-belt kecks and corduroy.

BOY

But like Humberside is Yorkshire still
and Lancashire is over the hill
and loneliness is Gaping Ghyll,
we never fought and we never will . . .

BOTH

'Cos you can do nothing wrong in my eyes.
You can do nothing wrong in my eyes.

BOY

Some go mental for pills and smokes,

GIRL

And some go sleeping with other blokes,

BOTH

But you can do nothing wrong in my eyes.

BOY

You took me in, with pillow talk and Bombay gin.

GIRL

You walked me home, I woke up naked and alone.

BOY

I plucked a rose, and strew the petals on your clothes.

GIRL

That rose was dead, it passed away behind the shed.

BOY

But like Humberside . . .

BOTH

'Cos you can do nothing wrong in my eyes.
You can do nothing wrong in my eyes.

BOY

Some go looking for tabs and wraps,

GIRL

And some go loafing with lesser lads,

BOTH

But you can do nothing wrong in my eyes.

BOY *(spoken):*

And when a scabby football's your only friend
It's just you against the gable end

287

Gig

GIRL (*spoken*):
Yeah, yeah, yeah . . .

BOY
You watch the dawn, and talk about the earth reborn.

GIRL
You watch the dusk, like watching iron turn to rust.

BOY
If looks could kill, they'd find me slaughtered on the hill.

GIRL
The day you laugh, I'd frame it in a photograph.

BOTH
But like Humberside . . .

BOTH
'Cos you can do nothing wrong in my eyes.
You can do nothing wrong in my eyes.

BOY
Some go hunting for thrills and flings,

GIRL
And some find fault in every little thing,

BOTH
But you can do nothing wrong in my eyes.

♫

The Scaremongers

Two Moons

I was a probation officer and my father was a probation officer before me. Not exactly the family business; more a case of him paving the way and me following in his footsteps. He did his training at Manchester University and twenty years later so did I. I was interviewed by the same man, very probably in the same office, very possibly sitting in the same chair. During my interview I talked seamlessly and with great conviction about public attitudes to offending, about recent legislation in the criminal justice system, about social policy and the welfare state, and about the role of the caring professions in advanced capitalist societies. After about half an hour the man taking notes leaned back in his swivel chair, put his hands behind his head and his feet on the bookshelf and said, 'OK, OK. Anyway, how's your dad?'

My father had applied to become a probation officer following a national recruitment drive. He saw an advert in the paper that said something like, 'Are you the kind of person who can make a difference to society?' Yes I am, he said to himself, and filled in the forms. There would be a rigorous selection process to whittle the numbers down from a great many to just a few, followed by two years of unpaid training and some pretty hefty essay writing. But even though my father had left school at fifteen (about three years after he'd started smoking) and had a young family to support, none of that seemed to dampen his optimism or blunt his confidence. He'd walk it, or at least talk his way through it. The phrase 'not backwards at coming forwards' could have been coined for my dad. An example: in those days, it was still acceptable for prospective employers to ask that applicants submit photographs of themselves. To most people applying to Greater Manchester Probation Service this meant a passport-size snapshot. But not to my dad, apparently. Inside his envelope he enclosed a 10 × 8 publicity shot, taken to promote his role as Jeff in Huddersfield Amateurs' production of *Brigadoon*. At that time, probation work was often about trying to strike a balance between care and control; some officers saw themselves as counsellors and social workers, others as law enforcers and agents of the courts. And Dad had obviously decided to nail his colours to the mast from the very outset, because in the crook of his elbow he was cradling a loaded rifle.

My dad retired from the service in 1994, six months after I did. I was thirty-one when I asked for my cards. It wasn't easy, walking out of a good job, especially at a time when there were no jobs. I was chucking away four years of training, a reasonable income and seven years of pension contributions – to become a poet. But maybe some strange synchronicity was at work. If my father hadn't made the big decision to join, then perhaps I would never have been able to make the big decision to leave.

Before he was a probation officer my father had been a fireman, like his father before him. He'd also been a plumber, a gardener, a mechanic, a driver, a salesman and an engineer. He still works occasionally, taking statements from prisoners in Strangeways for a firm of local solicitors, and most days in the summer he can be seen pushing the lawnmower across Hemplow bowling green, the thin, dew-soaked cuttings forming a neat little rainbow between the blades of the mower and the grass box, under the humped shoulder of Saddleworth Moor. Or he's up on the moor itself, in a big coat, with headphones over his ears, sweeping the ground in front of him with a second-hand metal detector, like a latter-day version of Wordsworth's leech-gatherer. But first and foremost my father is a performer. Always has been, always will be. He needs no more than an audience of one, but he's equally comfortable in front of the many thousands, perhaps hundreds of thousands of people who across the years have seen him act, dance, sing and tell tales. A born exaggerator, he prefaces his very tallest stories with the phrase 'And this is God's honest truth', and should further proof of veracity be needed, concludes with the words 'Isn't that right, Simjoss?' I don't know where this Scandinavian-sounding form of my name first originated (they once went to Norway on holiday – is that it?) but I've learned to like it, just as I've learned to nod my head when he finishes one of his yarns, thus sanctioning the authenticity of his hyperbole, no matter how improbable. My dad's performing repertoire also takes in after-dinner speaking, voice-over work, writing and directing plays and pantomimes, and presenting videos on local history (all five series available from Duncan's, the village barber, on display between the styptic pencils and Duralon combs). In fact it's fair to say that for the right size of backhander he is more or less permanently available for any job requiring a quick mind and a sharp tongue. He told me recently that to bring in a bit of extra cash when he was newly married he used to moonlight as a comedian at a nightclub in Barnsley. And telling jokes to a bunch of thirsty miners and their thirsty wives on a Friday night in South Yorkshire would have been no picnic.

> Me: 'I bet that was no picnic.'
> Him: 'Piece of cake.'

Knowing him as I do, on this occasion I'm prepared to believe that this is not just a case of God's honest truth, but a statement of fact.

Unlike colour blindness, which my father suffers from (red and green being the biggest problem – a nightmare at traffic lights), the propensity towards performance isn't restricted to the males of the family. Perhaps it's a gene, something in the blood, passed on from generation to generation. The Tudge, not yet eight years old, is already an aspiring comedienne, practising concert pianist, wannabe ballet dancer and would-be member of the Magic Circle. She's even appeared in her first radio drama for the BBC, even if it was only to giggle and say the word 'potatoes'. On top of all the clubs and classes she attends during the week, on Saturdays she stands in front of a full-length mirror above a shoeshop in Huddersfield, and for three hours an ageing local thespian teaches her and several dozen other young girls from the region how to show off. If theatricality were to be traced back along the branches and limbs of our family, the roots would

probably be located in the union of Harry Armitage and
Marjorie Kirby, my grandparents on my father's side.
Together they were among the founder members of
Marsden Operatic and Dramatic Society in 1926. The
society flourishes to this day; my grandmother starred in
their very first show, *The Mikado*, and a member of the
family has been involved in every musical production
since then, if not actually taking the spotlight then
showing people to their seats or typing up the programme. Harry was clearly a willing and capable participant – why else would he dress up as a very convincing
knight of the Crusades and smile for the camera? But I
get the feeling that Madge was the real driving force, and
there are any number of photographs in the family album
that bear witness to her reputation as an enthusiastic
amateur actor, sepia-tinted snaps of a familiar face dis-
guised by a long wig or thick make-up, often executing
some exaggerated movement or sweeping gesture. Anec-
dotal evidence, passed on in legend and lore, confirms
this theory. My mum tells a particularly believable tale
about first seeing her potential mother-in-law in the
church nativity play. During one scene, and with the kind
of gusto that would make the actual Annunciation look
like a visit from the postman, my grandmother apparently
leapt on to the stage, threw open her arms, and in a
voice somewhere between Joyce Grenfell and God himself
exclaimed to the whole of humanity, 'TWO MOONS
SHALL SEE HER TIME FULFILLED!' The phrase
'two moons' is now a well-established family catchphrase,
uttered under the breath and designed to puncture an
inflated ego.

So Dad took centre stage. And Mum, more comfortable selling raffle tickets than actually treading the boards, was nevertheless dragooned into many a village production. She was often in the chorus, rhubarbing and wasp-chewing with the other mums and daughters at the back of the stage, clicking her fingers, slapping her knees and swaying to the music. For my sins I inherited her red cheeks and her tendency to blush at the mildest discomfort, a condition I thought would pass with time, like acne, but which seems to have got worse with age, or possibly with drink. Mum remembered recently that when she was a child, the dustbin men who were going past the end of the garden had asked her name. 'Audrey,' she said. They burst into a chorus of 'Audrey Just Laughed and Laughed and Laughed', a popular music hall song of the time, apparently. And apparently Audrey did not laugh and laugh but ran into the house in tears and buried her head in her mother's lap. About thirty-five years later, Audrey's mother, my grandma Lily, sent me outside at five minutes to midnight with a piece of coal in my hands. As the only dark-haired person in the house I was going to be the first-footer – the first person to enter the house in the New Year – and would bring good luck with me. I was seven. I was wearing a pair of kung-fu pyjamas, very modish at the time, and it was snowing. A group of drunken men came down the road, singing dirty songs and throwing snowballs, and in my martial arts nightwear I must have looked like a good target. I bawled and banged on the door but they wouldn't open it until the clock had struck. Like Audrey, I did not laugh.

All the shows took place in the Parochial Hall. If I spent

my summers mooching around at the side of Huddersfield's cricket fields, trapping frogs in crisp packets and
arguing with my sister about whose turn it was to go on
the bike, I spent most of the winter hanging about in the
wings or under the stage of the Parochial Hall. Wherever
I went in that building, my dad's voice was never far
away, though always mutated into whatever part he happened to be playing that season, such as the persecuted
Jew Tevye in *Fiddler on the Roof*, or the Siamese king in
The King and I, or Mendoza the Bandit in *Viva Mexico* with
his dodgy goatee, beach-towel poncho and Benidorm
sombrero. He brought the parts home with him as well.
To learn his lines and to get into the role he had to live
with the character, and so did we therefore. One month
he was the wily Spaniard Sancho Panza, the next month
he was the clowning Roman servant Hysterium. He once
played Bill Sykes, the malicious and sadistic villain in
the musical *Oliver!* He grew a scary beard, developed a
mean-looking sneer and adopted a snarling, sharp-toothed
dog for the duration of the show, a nasty little bull terrier
with a black eye. Even though it was make-believe he
scared the bejesus out of most of the children in the cast,
even the cocky little kid playing the cocky little Artful
Dodger. Too young even to land a part as one of Fagin's
pickpockets, I hid behind my mum's billowing skirts in
the dressing room, not sure what to make of this evil
monster with his evil dog who was also my father. I had
similar misgivings a few years later when he played the
part of Jud Fry in the musical *Oklahoma!* Bitter and twisted,
Jud simmers and seethes in a dirty little smoke shack at
the bottom of the garden, dreaming of getting a proper

girl rather than making do with the pictures of Parisian ladies pinned to his wall. At one point, he tries to get his hands on a 'Little Wonder', a kaleidoscope with a spring-operated flick-knife incorporated into the mechanism. Curly, his love rival, attempts to convince Jud that people will only appreciate him if he commits suicide. 'That's a good-looking rope ya got there.' Eventually Jud falls on his own knife and dies. Then everyone's happy and goes on a picnic.

Aside from odd little walk-on parts as bellhops and chimney sweeps (and once as a waiter in *The Good Companions*, though why an eight-year-old boy would be serving Sauternes at the Ritz was never explained to me) my first real job with Marsden Operatic and Dramatic Society was as a call-boy. This much-coveted role had been vacated by my sister the previous year; having entered adolescence she now qualified as a dancing girl. The call-boy's job began with a general shout of 'overture and beginners' five minutes before the curtain went up. For the rest of the show, the task was to run between dressing rooms with a clipboard and a script, making sure members of the cast were not drinking cooking sherry by the fire exit but in position at the side of the stage ready to make their entrance. During lulls in the action I'd watch the performance from the wings or through pinholes in the backcloth, or whisper to the other people who populated the dimly lit crepuscular world of backstage – people who pulled curtains and threw switches or whacked two slats of wood together to imitate the sound of a gunshot. One of those people was the prompt, a woman who seemed to have been sitting on the same wooden stool for ever and a day, with a script in one hand and a cigarette in the other. It must have been an odd experience for the audience, not only *hearing* forgotten lines being barked from the wings, but *seeing* them as well, as they arrived on stage in a discharge of exhaled smoke. This was in the days before the phrase 'health and safety' had ever been thought of and when 'fire regulations' meant a bucket of sand by the back door, usually full of stubbed-out fags.

The job of call-boy in a church hall not much bigger than an indoor tennis court shouldn't have been too complicated, but my father's house has many mansions. The women's dressing room was situated in the kitchen. In amongst the warming drawers and work surfaces it was all bosoms and frills, with many mirrors stacked against the sinks and tables, so the false eyelashes and acres of powdered flesh were reflected to infinity. There wasn't much room; sometimes, to try and find the leading lady or one of the dancers, I'd have to push through a rail of clothes. It was like going through the back of the wardrobe, leaving the everyday world behind and popping out in a land of bloomers and corsets, a sort of parallel universe where women of the village had morphed into their exotic doppelgängers, into princesses or chambermaids or cowgirls or nuns. In fact it's only with hindsight that I realize why the role of call-boy could only be trusted to the prepubescent. Members of the WI strutted about in high heels and feather boas. The mothers of my friends in leopard-skin leotards and fishnet stockings giggled and gossiped around a large tin of Quality Street. My Sunday school teacher, struggling to lace some convoluted corset or basque, turned the freckled canvas of her naked back towards me and asked me to lend a hand. At first I knocked before entering, but after a while I stopped knocking, and no one seemed to mind. In fact no one seemed to notice.

The men were either skulking under the stage, like convicts in the lower deck of a transport ship en route to Botany Bay, or were billeted in various outbuildings round the back of the hall. To enter those areas was to walk in on a card school or a drinking game or the punchline of some stupendously filthy joke. Not that the dressing rooms were always divided along gender lines. During the society's 1976 performance of the dodgy musical *Showboat* the spirit of apartheid suddenly visited itself upon that little corner of West Yorkshire, with the white supremacists being accommodated in the centrally heated kitchen, and the blacked-up 'Negroes' being segregated in a defunct railway carriage in the car park with a few rugs on the floor and condensation dripping from the roof. In fairness, there was probably some sound practical reason for this ghettoization, but for the sake of a good story I'm prepared to overlook it. What cannot be overlooked, however, was the nickname given to the railway carriage, which even in these days of truth and reconciliation I am not inclined to put into print. Occasionally, remembering this unfortunate epithet, the phrase will be whispered by some long-serving member of the society, but usually within inverted commas, and accompanied by a facial expression meaning 'Did we really use to say that?'

★

In these more enlightened times I don't imagine that the Palladium Theatre in London insists on such segregation, and as we hang around the stage door after *The Sound of Music*, there's no indication that members of the Third Reich are being given the star treatment in a sumptuous dressing room while the persecuted and fugitive Austrians are slumming it outside in a Portakabin. We're here because of the Tudge. She's watched the whole series of *How Do You Solve a Problem Like Maria?*, and now she's seen the show, and now she's hoping to catch a glimpse of Connie Fisher, her heroine. In anticipation of this hoped-for meeting, the Tudge is wearing an enormous pink coat made from synthetic fur, white tights and a pair of ballet shoes. She looks like she's on her way to a fancy dress party got up as a stick of candyfloss. Her mum's dressed to the nines as well, and together they wait by the big iron railings and heavy iron gate, not prepared to give up their position at the front of the queue or let go of the possibility of a photograph, or an autograph, or even the touch of a hand. I'm a little off to one side. It probably looks like I'm some killjoy dad who wouldn't be seen dead queuing for an autograph ('Miserable sod, looking down his nose. Quite happy to scrawl his *own* name in some rubbishy book of poems' blah blah blah), but I'm not, honestly, I'm sheltering in a doorway because it's raining and it's December and it's getting late, and I'm busting for a pee, and as Lesley Garrett emerges from the theatre to spread happiness and thanks around the crowd of onlookers, I see my chance and slip off to the underground toilet at the top end of Carnaby Street.

There are two dossers sleeping on the floor of the poorly lit subterranean urinal, or not sleeping at all, as it turns out, but waiting, because when I've finished doing what I need to do and turn around, one of them is standing in front of me. He has a hood over his head, though of course down here it isn't raining.

'*Big Issue*, mate?' he says.

His hands are stuffed in the pouch-pocket at the front of his sweatshirt. I look for a bundle of magazines, either stacked on the floor or in a bag around his neck, but there aren't any magazines to be seen. It doesn't seem to bother him that as a vendor he has nothing to offer. In fact he seems quite liberated by the idea, almost aggressively confident, and suddenly, through the rapidly thinning membrane of alcohol, I get the picture. This is a one-way transaction. I'm not being mugged exactly, but the under-lying suggestion is that I should stump up and should not expect a copy of the aforementioned publication in return. I have a sudden flash of memory, pulling up in a car with my father in one of the side streets around Maine Road. Why, in God's name, were we going to watch Manchester City? Anyhow, we get out of the car and up comes this big scary lad in an anorak and bovver boots and says to my dad, 'Fifty pence to look after your car, mister.' Fifty pence sounds like about ten years' pocket money to me, so I must have been about nine or ten. My dad looks up the road, then down the road, then back up the road, like he's practising the Green Cross Code, then he puts his face in the face of the boy in the coat and the big boots and says to him, 'I'm a policeman, son. I don't need my car looking after.' Of course he isn't a policeman at all, he's a plumber, or he's a fireman, or a gardener or a mechanic or possibly even a trainee or even a fully fledged probation officer by this time. But he's also an actor, and a bullshitter, and a bloody good one. He's also been playing Police Officer Shranke in *West Side Story* for Halifax Light Opera, and if he doesn't take any backchat from the Puerto Rican hoodlums of Manhattan he sure as hell doesn't take it from some oikish petty criminal in south Manchester. 'I'm a policeman,' he says, and the boy believes him. I know he believes him, because when we return to the car two hours later both wing mirrors are missing, the aerial is tied in a knot and there's a blob of chewing gum stuck in the lock, which is what happened to coppers who parked their cars in Moss Side in the early seventies. If we'd been regular citizens we'd have probably got away with a missing hubcap. Obviously I'm remembering this incident because thirty-some years later in a public toilet in London I'd like to be able to stick my face into the face of the chancer in front of me and say, 'I'm a copper, son, I don't buy non-existent magazines.' I'd probably like to throw in a 'So beat it, punk' as well. But I don't. I don't have the neck. I don't have the balls. Neither do I have a boy at my side thinking, Go on, stick it to him, Dad. What I do have is a wife and daughter up there on the pavement, who wouldn't be too pleased to see me emerging from beneath the pavement with a bloody nose or worse. I also have a banknote in my pocket – a fiver, I hope – but in the quick handover between my sweaty palm and his twitchy fingers there isn't time to examine the denomination. Halfway towards the light at the top of the stairs it does occur to me to turn around and shout, 'And you can keep the change.' But if this is my line, I fluff it.

When I get back, flashbulbs are flashing, and in the middle of a polite scrum of excited people, kindly, wholesome Connie Fisher has her long, elegant arm around a seven-year-old girl who happens to be our daughter. Speedy Sue shoots with the camera. Sweetheart Connie even offers to pose for a second shot, just in case she was blinking in the first one. Having not only been touched but cuddled, and with an autographed programme in her handbag, the Tudge is finally persuaded away from the spotlight, and falls asleep over my shoulder in a crowded Tube train full of swaying drunks. What's interesting about the photograph, examining it more closely, is the look on the Tudge's face. Not a Giaconda smile exactly, but certainly an expression that can work in two directions. On the one hand she's thinking, This is me having my picture taken with Connie off the telly. On the other hand, she might be thinking, This is Connie off the telly, having her photo taken with ME.

Two moons shall see her time fulfilled. In the soap operas, the old generation moves aside to make way for the next, sometimes in the same episode, sometimes at exactly the same moment in time. In Marsden, two cars leave the chapel of rest and pull out on to the main road, the body of Marjorie Armitage in the first, the remainder of the family in the stretch hearse that follows. Ahead of the cortège, the undertaker walks at a measured pace, his hat under his arm, his gloves folded across his hand. The people in the village, Marsdeners, stop whatever they're doing and nod, paying their respects. My grandmother was ninety-seven when she died – may she finally rest in peace. Sitting next to me on the cracked leather seat is the Tudge, the youngest of the Armitages. If, in later life, she decides to observe the tradition of a wife taking her husband's surname, she's also the last of the Armitages, and if tradition means doing what your ancestors did, i.e. performing at every available opportunity, then she's a very traditional girl. She is not resting in peace. She is bored out of her tiny mind.

> The Tudge: Dad, can we play I Spy?
> The father: I don't think so.
> The Tudge: Please, Dad. P-l-e-a-s-e?
> The father: OK then.
> The Tudge: I spy, with my little eye, something beginning with G.
> The father: Grass?
> The Tudge: No.
> The mother: Garage?
> The Tudge: No. Shall I give you a clue?
> The father: Go on then.
> The Tudge: Well, she just died and she's in that box.

After the crematorium we go back to the club with the family, all the branches of the tree, many offshoots, some I don't even recognize. Then we get the photographs out. Weddings. Holidays. People on the beach. Bridlington. Blackpool. Shows my grandmother appeared in: *The Country Girl*, *Our Miss Gibbs*, *The Girls of Gottenberg*, *No, No, Nanette*. Photographs of relatives, some half remembered, some completely forgotten, some long dead. 'Who's that?' the Tudge wants to know. 'And who's that? And who's that?' Sticky fingers on fading celluloid. Then they cover the snooker table with a thick roll of canvas and out comes the supper: sandwiches, vol-au-vents, pork pie, cake. My dad gives a speech. Not a long one but a big one, from the heart. No embroidery necessary. No confirmation required from Simjoss. A few tears. Handshakes and hugs. In the far room someone drops the jackpot on the bandit. Money behind the bar. We talk some more, and we drink some more. Then we tell tales. And then – what she would have wanted – we sing.